CASES IN INTERNATIONAL FINANCIAL REPORTING STANDARDS

3rd Edition

GW00566544

CASES IN INTERNATIONAL FINANCIAL REPORTING STANDARDS

3rd Edition

Derry Cotter, FCA

Published by
Chartered Accountants Ireland
Chartered Accountants House
47–49 Pearse Street
Dublin 2
www.charteredaccountants.ie

The opinions expressed in this publication are those of the author and do not necessarily represent the views of Chartered Accountants Ireland. The text is designed to provide accurate and authoritative information in regard to the subject matter covered. It is sold on the understanding that Chartered Accountants Ireland is not engaged in rendering professional services. If professional advice or other expert assistance is required, the services of a competent professional should be sought.

ISBN: 978-1-908199-43-0

First published 2008
Second edition 2009
Third edition 2012

Typeset by Compuscript
Printed by Turner's Printing

To the students of Chartered Accountants Ireland and UCC, whose courtesy and kindness has made teaching such a great pleasure

TABLE OF CONTENTS
(With Case Study Topics)

Page

Page

INTRODUCTION

The Case Study Approach

It is generally perceived that the use of case study material significantly enhances student learning. Case studies are seen as an invaluable educational resource, one that is entirely complementary to other methods of teaching. Where conventional textbooks typically provide a discipline's core knowledge material, case studies can assist in developing the students' critical and analytical skills, and enhance their capacity for problem-solving. This is often achieved by presenting challenging scenarios, which require the students to integrate and apply the material contained in conventional texts.

The Aim of this Book

Cases in International Financial Reporting Standards offers a broad range of case study material in the area of international financial reporting standards. Each case provides many examples of how the International Accounting Standards (IAS) and the International Financial Reporting Standards (IFRS) are applied in practice. The book is targeted both at accounting practitioners and at undergraduate students who have completed an introductory course in Financial Reporting, as well as those preparing for examinations set by the professional accountancy bodies. From a lecturer's perspective, it is envisaged that this case study book would provide an ideal tutorial pack.

Cases in International Financial Reporting Standards offers a range of case study material in the core areas of financial reporting. Several case examples focus on *Reporting Financial Performance*, with coverage of key issues such as the presentation of financial statements, earnings per share, interim financial reporting, share-based payment, non-current assets held for sale and discontinued operations, accounting policies, events after the reporting period, leases, revenue, employee benefits, the effects of changes in foreign exchange rates, related party disclosures, operating segments and financial instruments. There is extensive coverage of *Accounting for Assets*, which includes inventories, construction contracts, property, plant and equipment, asset impairment and intangible assets. There is also a focus on *Accounting for Liabilities* such as income taxes, and provisions and contingent liabilities. Finally, many aspects of *Group Accounts* are addressed, including business combinations and investments in associates and joint ventures.

Tips and guidance for using this book

Two indexes are provided to facilitate quick and easy access to material:

- The first, at the front of the book, identifies the case study questions in which *specific IASs or IFRSs* are addressed.

- The second index, which is at the back of the book, provides an alphabetical listing, *by subject topic,* referenced to the case study questions.

- The cases are set at a level that assumes that student users will have completed an introductory course in financial reporting.

- The cases are written so that they can be used in an open-book environment, whereby students can refer to their own notes and other sources of information when preparing their answer.

- Past FAE Financial Reporting papers, included in the 3rd edition, have been updated to fully reflect all subsequent changes in IFRS.

ACKNOWLEDGEMENTS

I wish to thank Michael Diviney for commissioning the 3rd edition of this book. I also want to acknowledge the invaluable administrative support provided by Agnieszka Pobedynska.

I am especially indebted to David Ahern and Brendan Doyle, for their insightful comments and suggestions. Any errors or omissions, however, are entirely the responsibility of the author.

Index to Case Studies

Reference is to Case Study *Question*

Topic	Darcy	Rocket	Telfer	Campbell
Conceptual framework				
IFRS 1				
IFRS 2				
IFRS 3			(A) (i) & (A) (ii)	
IFRS 5			(B)	
IFRS 8				(3)
IFRS 9				
IFRS 10			(A) (iii) + (c) (i)	
IFRS 11	(a) (ii)			
IAS 1				
IAS 2	(b) (iii)	(a) (i) – (a) (iii)		
IAS 8				
IAS 10				
IAS 11				
IAS 12				
IAS 16			(B)	
IAS 17	(b) (i)	(a) (iv)		
IAS 18	(b) (ii)		(D) (i) & (D) (ii)	
IAS 19				(2)
IAS 20	(b) (iv)			
IAS 21				
IAS 23		(b) (i)	(c)	
IAS 24			(C) (ii)	
IAS 27				
IAS 28	(a) (i) + (a) (ii)			
IAS 33				(1)
IAS 34				(3)
IAS 36		(b) (i)		
IAS 37				
IAS 38				
IAS 39				
IAS 40				

BELLMOTH GROUP

You are the audit senior in a firm of Chartered Accountants and Registered Auditors, Goodman Hart and Co. You are currently reviewing the draft consolidated financial statements of Bellmoth Holdings Limited and its subsidiary companies, Caterpillar Limited and Butterfly Limited.

Your Firm's audit partner, Yvonne Russell, has sent you a memo containing the following information:

- Background to the group companies: Appendix I below

- Matters arising from the 2x05
  audit of the group: Appendix II below
- Draft consolidated statement of
  financial position and statement
  of comprehensive income for the group: Appendix III below

Requirement:

On the basis of the information provided by Yvonne Russell, draft a memorandum to her outlining:
- Recommendations as to how the accounting issues arising should be dealt with. You should include an explanation of your reasons for the proposed accounting treatment.
- The journal entries necessary to adjust the draft financial statements.
- Disclosure requirements (outline *not* detailed notes) relating *only* to Caterpillar's investment in Bumble Bee (see matters arising, below).

Note: You are *not* required to redraft the financial statements.

50 marks

Appendix I

Background to the Group Companies

The Bellmoth Group comprises the following companies:

Bellmoth Holdings Limited (Bellmoth) – A holding company employing 16 people and providing services to the other group trading companies.

Caterpillar Limited – A 100% subsidiary of Bellmoth, acquired several years ago. Caterpillar is a major supplier of food products, employing 220 staff located throughout the major cities in Ireland.

Butterfly Limited – Butterfly was established in the United States on 1 January 2x05 by Bellmoth. Butterfly manufactures high quality carpets to customers' specifications. The company, which employs 100 staff, is an 80% subsidiary of Bellmoth. It operates on an autonomous basis, only referring to Bellmoth in relation to matters of strategic importance.

Appendix II

Matters Arising from the 2x05 Audit of the Bellmoth Group

(1) Caterpillar

(i)   *Restructuring*

In October 2x05 Caterpillar announced that it was investigating the possibility of rationalising its provision of foodstuffs with a short shelf life. Following a feasibility study, a detailed plan was drawn up in December for the sale of surplus non-current assets, and for the redeployment of staff. The plan has been approved in principle by members of staff who will be affected.

It has been estimated that the downsizing of short life foodstuff sales would necessitate a provision of €2 million at 31 December 2x05. This provision is analysed as follows;

	€'000
Loss on disposal of non-current assets	650
Redundancy settlements	350
Warehouse re-design costs	220

Marketing costs to refocus company's sales promotion on continuing lines	380
Future operating losses of short-life foodstuffs sales	400
	2,000

No provision has been made in the financial statements at 31 December 2x05.

(ii)   *Warranty provisions and refunds*

- It is estimated that the discounted value of future warranty claims against goods supplied by the company during 2x05 amounts to €1.5 million at 31 December 2x05.

- Additionally, Caterpillar has a policy of making cash refunds or exchanging goods at their customers' request. Although there is no legal obligation to do so, it is believed that the policy has promoted a greater than average level of customer loyalty to the company.

  On the basis of past experience, it is estimated that cash refunds relating to 2x05 sales will amount to €800,000 in 2x06. Additionally, it is estimated that €200,000 of goods sold in 2x05 will be exchanged in 2x06. Caterpillar earns an average gross margin of 50% on sales.

  No provisions have been made in the draft 2x05 accounts, either in respect of warranty provisions or refunds.

(iii)   *Staff retraining costs*

Legislative changes at European level during 2x05 have resulted in more stringent requirements relating to product design. Consequently, staff retraining costs over the next three years are estimated as follows:

	€'000
2x06	300
2x07	400
2x08	500

(iv)   Joint venture

On 1 January 2x05, Caterpillar set up Bumble Bee as a joint venture initiative with Thompson Products Limited. Caterpillar obtained a 50% stake in Bumble Bee and, along with Thompson Products Ltd, participated actively in the company's financial strategy and day-to-day running.

Caterpillar's investment in Bumble Bee cost €1 million, which was financed by a term loan. Caterpillar paid €20,000 to an adviser, who researched alternative sources of finance on the company's behalf, and administrative fees of €25,000 were charged by the bank.

Caterpillar made sales amounting to €1 million to Bumble Bee during 2x05, on which the profit margin was 30%. Of these sales, half were still held in inventory by Bumble Bee at 31 December 2x05.

Bumble Bee had sales of €5 million, and cost of sales of €2 million for the year ended 31 December 2x05. The company's operating profit was €1.4 million, all of which was retained.

With the exception of the sales by Caterpillar to Bumble Bee, no entries have been made by Caterpillar (or in the draft consolidated financial statements) in respect of its investment in the joint venture.

(v)   Tangible non-current assets

- On 1 January 2x04 Caterpillar purchased a block of land for €600,000. The land was revalued at €800,000 at 31 December 2x04, and was sold during 2x05 for €1.3 million. The disposal has not been reflected in the draft 2x05 financial statements, and the land continues to be included in tangible non-current assets at a valuation of €800,000.

- On 1 January 2x03 Caterpillar purchased a commercial property for investment purposes. The property, which cost €500,000, was included in the Statement of Financial Position at its fair value of €700,000 at 31 December 2x04. During 2x05 a rezoning decision had reduced the value of the property to €300,000. No account of the rezoning decision has been taken in preparing the 2x05 draft financial statements.

(2) Butterfly

Inventory
Butterfly purchased inventories of wool over the last quarter of 2x05 as
follows:

Month	Tons purchased	Cost per ton	Tons in inventory at end of month
Oct	10	$50,000	8
Nov	11	$60,000	15
Dec	9	$70,000	17

In accordance with normal accounting practice in the United States, the
closing inventory of wool has been valued on a LIFO basis, and this basis
has been applied in the draft consolidated financial statements.

The normal valuation basis in the Bellmoth Group is FIFO. The net realisable value of the wool at 31 December 2x05 was $30,000 per ton.

The rate of exchange at 31 December 2x05 was €1 = $1.50, and this was
also the rate throughout the last quarter of the year.

Appendix III

Draft Consolidated Financial Statements

Draft Statement of Comprehensive Income
for the Year Ended 31 December 2x05

	€'000
Revenue	36,800
Cost of sales	(18,600)
Gross profit	18,200
Distribution costs	(4,800)
Administrative expenses	(3,900)
Other expenses	(1,500)
Finance costs	(300)
Profit before tax	7,700
Income tax expense	(700)
Profit for the year from continuing operations	7,000
Other comprehensive income:	
Items that will not be reclassified to profit or loss:	
Gains on property revaluation	450
Total comprehensive income for the year	7,450
Profit attributable to:	
Owners of the parent	6,200
Non-controlling interests	800
	7,000
Total comprehensive income attributable to:	
Owners of the parent	6,650
Non-controlling interests	800
	7,450

Draft Statement of Financial Position as at 31 December 2x05

	Notes	2x05 €'000	2x04 €'000
Assets			
Non-current assets			
Property, plant and equipment		18,000	
Goodwill		14,000	
		32,000	
Current assets			
Inventories		9,000	
Trade and other receivables		5,000	
Cash and cash equivalents		3,000	
		17,000	
Total assets		49,000	
Liabilities			
Current liabilities			
Trade and other payables		9,500	
Current tax payable		1,000	
		10,500	
		10,500	
Non-current liabilities			
Convertible debentures		2,000	
10% Preference shares		300	
Provisions		5,500	
Other payables		6,000	
		13,800	
Total liabilities		24,300	
Net assets		24,700	
Equity			
Capital and reserves attributable to equity			
Holders of the Parent			
Share capital		600	
Share premium account		4,800	
Revaluation reserve		1,200	
Retained earnings		14,800	
		21,400	
Non-controlling interests		3,300	
Total equity		24,700	

CROMPTON PLANT AND FERTILISER GROUP

The Crompton Plant and Fertiliser Group comprises Crompton Holdings Limited and its subsidiary companies which it has held for several years. Only one subsidiary, Ingston Limited, in which Crompton Holdings Limited holds 90% of the equity shares, is not wholly owned. In your capacity as Group Financial Accountant you are currently reviewing the draft consolidated accounts of the group. The Finance Director has requested that you prepare a memorandum outlining any issues which may require amendment. The financial statements are being authorised by the Board of Directors on 20 July 2x06.

In its separate financial statements, Crompton Holdings accounts at cost for investments in subsidiaries.

(1) Acquisition of Plant Life Limited

On 31 May 2x06 the parent company, Crompton Holdings Limited, acquired 100% of Plant Life Limited. The group has regularly purchased goods from Plant Life Limited in each of the last five years (purchases amounted to €2.5 million in the year ended 31 May 2x06), and the acquisition was seen as being strategic in copper-fastening the Group's presence in the residential market for house plants.

Consideration for the acquisition comprised the following:

- 1 million €1 equity shares of Crompton Holdings Limited. The market value of these shares on 31 May 2x06 was €6 each.

- 100,000 shares in Grafton Bank Plc which had been purchased as an investment by Crompton Holdings on 1 October 2x05 for €1 million. The market value of these shares at 31 May 2x06 was €1.35

million, though the increase in value has not been reflected in the financial statements.

- Cash consideration of €400,000, payable on 1 June 2x08, which is contingent on certain profitability parameters being achieved by Plant Life Limited over the next two years. At 31 May 2x06 the directors of Crompton Limited were confident that this consideration would not become payable, but a new contract awarded to the company on the 1 July 2x06 means that the required profitability targets are likely to be achieved. Borrowed funds are normally available to Crompton Holdings Limited at 10% per annum.

No entries have been made in the consolidated accounts, or the accounts of Crompton Holdings Limited, relating to this consideration.

Having requested additional details relating to the new subsidiary, the following information is brought to your attention:

(i) The draft financial statements of Plant Life Limited for the year ended 31 May 2x06 are included in Appendix I.

(ii) At 31 May 2x06 the finished goods inventory of Plant Life Limited was valued on a first-in first-out basis. The goods were subsequently sold for €200,000 less than their value in the statement of financial position at 31 May 2x06.

(iii) At a Board meeting in November 2x05, the Directors of Plant Life Limited had committed the Company to a reorganisation programme costing €250,000, which commenced in June 2x06. No provision has been made for these costs in the financial statements at 31 May 2x06. This will also result in the immediate disposal of machinery for €300,000, net of selling costs. These machines had a net book value of €400,000 at 31 May 2x06. Negotiations with the Board of Crompton Holdings Limited commenced in January 2x06.

(iv) Crompton Holdings Limited has incurred professional fees of €100,000 relating to the acquisition of Plant Life Limited. No provision has been made for these expenses, which are payable in August 2x06. Additionally, general management expenses amounting to €85,000 have been included in other receivables in the consolidated financial statements of the Crompton Group at 31 May 2x06. It is intended to treat these expenses as part of the cost of acquiring Plant Life Limited.

(v) In February 2x06 Plant Life Limited took a legal action against one of its suppliers, on the basis that goods supplied were faulty. An amount of €100,000 was included under trade and other receivables at 31 May 2x06, as the minimum amount of the gain expected from this action. On 28 June 2x06, Plant Life received a settlement of €320,000 from the supplier in respect of its claim. The financial statements of the group are due to be authorised for issue on 20 July 2x06.

(vi) The fair value of the land and buildings of Plant Life Limited at 31 May 2x06 was €2.5 million. Buildings have not been depreciated as their residual value is expected to exceed their cost price.

(vii) A dividend of €600,000 was paid by Plant Life Limited in July 2x06 out of profits of the year ended 31 May 2x06. This was **not** provided for in the financial statements at 31 May 2x06.

(2) Group Accounts

The Group Accounts have also been prepared in draft form (see Appendix II below). These accounts do *not* include the new subsidiary Plant Life Limited. The following accounting issue relating to the group accounts has not been fully resolved:

On 1 June 2x05 Ingston Limited commenced the construction of a leisure centre for the Company's employees. The premises were completed in May 2x06 at a total cost of €3 million. It has been agreed by the trustees of the employees' pension scheme that the cost of the building will be offset against a deficit on the fund, which has been accrued as a provision in the Group financial statements at 31 May 2x06.

Ingston Limited has the full use of the property for the next five years, at which point ownership will transfer to the pension fund. A five-year contract has been signed with a leisure company for the rental of the centre at a net annual rent of €120,000, the first instalment being payable on 31 May 2x07.

The property has been included as an investment property in Ingston Limited's financial statements at 31 May 2x06 at its fair value of €4 million.

Appendix I

Draft Financial Statements of Plant Life Limited

Draft Statement of Comprehensive Income for the year ended 31 May 2x06

	2x06 €'000	2x05 €'000
Revenue	11,800	
Cost of sales	(7,950)	
Gross profit	3,850	
Distribution costs	(300)	
Administrative expenses	(500)	
Other expenses	(400)	
Finance costs	(400)	
Profit before tax	2,550	
Income tax expense	(1370)	
Profit for the year from continuing operations	1,180	
Other comprehensive income:		
Items that will not be reclassified to profit or loss:		
Gains on property revaluation	250	
Total comprehensive income for the year	1,430	

Draft Statement of Financial Position of Plant Life Limited
at 31 May 2x06

	Notes	2x06 €'000	2x05 €'000
Assets			
Non-current assets			
Land and buildings		2,298	
Plant and equipment		4,645	
		6,943	
Current assets			
Inventories of finished goods		1,469	
Trade and other receivables		1,395	
Cash and cash equivalent		1,155	
		4,019	
Total assets		10,962	
Liabilities			
Current liabilities			
Trade and other payables		2,215	
Income tax payable		1,350	
		3,565	
Non-current liabilities			
Term loan		820	
Provisions		300	
		1,120	
Total liabilities		4,685	
Net assets		6,277	
Equity			
Share capital		100	
Share premium account		250	
Revaluation surplus		1,000	
Retained earnings		4,927	
Total equity		6,277	

Appendix II

Draft Consolidated Financial Statements of the Crompton Group

**Draft Consolidated Statement of Comprehensive Income
for the year ended 31 May 2x06**

	2x06 €'000	2x05 €'000
Revenue	52,000	
Cost of sales	(27,950)	
Gross profit	24,050	
Distribution costs	(4,800)	
Administrative expenses	(9,500)	
Finance costs	(1,240)	
Gain on revaluation of investment property	1,000	
Profit before tax	8,130	
Income tax expense	(2,150)	
Profit for the year from continuing operations	5,980	
Other comprehensive income:		
Items that will not be reclassified to profit or loss:		
Gains on property revaluation	720	
Total comprehensive income for the year	6,700	
Profit attributable to:		
Owners of the parent	5,480	
Non-controlling interests	500	
	5,980	
Total comprehensive income attributable to:		
Owners of the parent	6,200	
Non-controlling interests	500	
	6,700	

Draft Statement of Financial Position of the Crompton Group at 31 May 2x06

	Notes	2x06 €'000	2x05 €'000
Assets			
Non-current assets			
Property, plant and equipment		31,550	
Investment Property		4,000	
		35,550	
Current assets			
Inventories		3,444	
Investments		1,000	
Trade and other receivables		3,395	
Cash and cash equivalents		2,155	
		9,994	
Total assets		45,544	
Liabilities			
Current liabilities			
Trade and other payables		6,965	
Income tax payable		4,150	
		11,115	
Non-current liabilities			
Convertible debentures		1,600	
Term loan		2,120	
Provisions		3,400	
		7,120	
Total liabilities		18,235	
Net assets		27,309	
Equity			
Equity attributable to owners of the parent			
Holders of the Parent			
Share capital		1,000	
Share premium account		1,700	
Revaluation surplus		3,904	
Other reserves		900	
Retained earnings		19,205	
		26,709	
Non-controlling interests		600	
Total equity		27,309	

Appendix III

Crompton Holdings: Group Structure

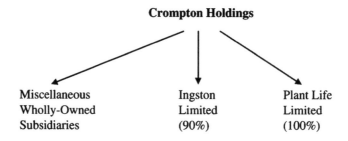

Crompton Holdings

| Miscellaneous Wholly-Owned Subsidiaries | Ingston Limited (90%) | Plant Life Limited (100%) |

Requirement:

You are required to draft a memorandum to the Finance Director of the Crompton Group, outlining your recommendations in respect of the accounting issues relating to:

(a)   Plant Life Limited
(b)   The Group

You are also required to show the calculation of goodwill relating to the acquisition of Plant Life Limited.

Your recommendations should be in accordance with generally accepted accounting practice.

The capital gains tax rate for all companies in the Group is 20%.

CURRENT ISSUES GROUP

The Current Issues Group has a major presence in the newspaper industry. You have recently been appointed as Group Financial Accountant, having worked with a competitor company for a number of years. Your appointment has come at a busy time, as the group is currently reviewing its accounts for the year ended 31 December 2x05.

In their separate/individual financial statements, all companies within the group account at cost for investments in subsidiaries, joint ventures and associates.

The following investments have been made in recent years;

(1) On 1 January 2x02, Current Issues acquired 80% of Big Times Limited at a cost of €800,000. The fair value of the net identifiable assets of Big Times at the date of acquisition was €500,000. The fair value of non-controlling interests was €120,000, and this was the basis on which non-controlling interests were measured at the acquisition date.

(2) During 2x05 Current Issues acquired 25% of the equity share capital of Sometimes Limited. Current Issues has representation on the Board of Directors of Sometimes Limited, and exercises significant influence over its financial policy decisions.

(3) On 31 March 2x05 Current Issues acquired 75% of the equity share capital of Blow the Whistle Limited, the consideration being equal to the fair value of the identifiable net assets acquired by Current Issues. Non-controlling interests at the acquisition date were measured at their proportionate share of the identifiable net assets of Blow the Whistle Limited.

Inter-company sales from Current Issues to Blow the Whistle during 2x05 amounted to €600,000, 30% of these arising during the first three months of the year.

(4) On 1 January 2x05 Current Issues purchased 80% of the equity share capital of Worthit Limited for €450,000. The fair value of the net identifiable assets of Worthit Limited at that time was €700,000, analysed as follows:

	€'000
Machinery	600
Inventory	350
Creditors	(250)
	700

Non-controlling interests at acquisition date were measured at the proportionate share of the fair value of the net assets acquired.

Accounting transactions

The following transactions occurred during the year ended 31 December 2x05:

(a) Related party issues

(i) On 31 March 2x05, Current Issues gave a loan of €1 million to one of its directors, Mr Smith. The purpose of the loan was to assist Mr Smith in repairing subsidence damage to his house.

(ii) On 8 May 2x05, Current Issues sold a printing press to Big Times at less than half its market value of €2.5million. On the same date, Sometimes made a gift of an old printing press, which had a market value of €1 million, to Big Times.

(iii) During 2x05 Sometimes Limited bought a large quantity of dye from Fine Tune Limited, which is owned by Tom Osborne, whose wife Margaret is the controlling shareholder of Sometimes Limited.

(b) Sale of assets

(i) On 1 January 2x05 Current Issues sold freehold land to Money Limited, a wholly-owned subsidiary of an investment bank. The land, which had cost €600,000 in 2x01, was sold for €700,000. Money Limited had an option to resell the land to Current Issues for €931,700 on 31 December 2x06. Current Issues had a call option to repurchase the land on the same basis.

(ii) On 1 January 2x02 Current Issues purchased freehold buildings for €300,000. The buildings were revalued to €500,000 in the financial statements at 31 December 2x03, and were sold for €600,000 in

March 2x05. It is group policy to depreciate buildings over 50 years on a straight line basis. A full year's depreciation is charged in the year of purchase, and no depreciation is charged in the year of disposal.

(c) *Financing*

 (i) On 1 January 2x05 Current Issues entered into a joint venture with Money Limited. A new company was set up, Fudgeit Limited, in which both Current Issues and Money held 50% of the shares. Under the terms of the joint venture agreement Money advanced a loan of €500,000 to Fudgeit, which was used to buy new equipment which is currently being used by Current Issues until Fudgeit begins trading. Current Issues has a majority of the Board members in Fudgeit, and has the power over decision-making in that company.

  Fudgeit Limited is included in the financial statements of the Group, using the equity method.

 (ii) On 30 September 2x05, Current Issues signed an agreement with Advance Factors. The following details are available:

- Advance Factors would give Current Issues an advance equal to 75% of its gross trade receivables. These funds were advanced primarily on a non-recourse basis, although Current Issues would be liable for the first €10,000 of bad debts. The normal level of bad debts incurred by Current Issues amounts to 3% of gross debtors.
- A facility fee of 1% of funds advanced would be charged.
- A fee equal to 1.5% of sales invoiced would be charged by Advance Factors in connection with the operation of the sales ledger of Current Issues.
- Interest at 12% per annum would be charged on funds advanced.
- At 31 December 2x05, Current Issues had received advances of €750,000 from Advance Factors, gross debtors standing at €1 million on that date. The following expenses were correctly accrued: interest €12,000, facility fee €7,500 and sales ledger fees of €30,000.

(d) *Titles*

Over the years Current Issues had expended large sums in promoting the group's titles. At 31 December 2x04 Current Issues had included

€450,000 in the Statement of Financial Position as an intangible asset in respect of these titles. An additional amount of €100,000 was also capitalised, this being the cost of titles procured from No Time Limited which had gone into liquidation during 2x04.

(e) *Impairment of assets*

In January 2x01 Current Issues had set up a division within the company to investigate the direction of the group's strategy in dealing with the rapid technological advances in the industry. Significant investment was made in developing an e-learning division. By 2x05 it had become clear that the e-learning division would become an insignificant market player. In accordance with IAS 36 *Impairment of Assets*, an impairment review of the e-learning division was carried out at 31 December 2x05.

(i)

	Book value of net assets of division in Statement of Financial Position	*Fair value less costs to sell of net assets of division*
	€'000	**€'000**
	1,200*	500

	€'000
Goodwill	300
Generic software development	400
Tangible non-current assets carried at cost less accumulated depreciation	500
	1,200*

(ii) Value in use

Efforts are currently in progress to convert the e-learning division to a commercially viable database. This work is at an advanced stage, and the results are extremely promising. The following information is available in respect of the value in use of the net assets of the division:

The cumulative values of future cash flows of the division at 31 December 2x10 are estimated as follows. These figures are based on the company's approved budgets for the next five years.

	€'000
Total cash flows from operations before taxation	2,830*
Software development costs	(2,000)
Finance costs	(1,000)

*This figure includes inflows of €1,400,000 which will result from planned development expenditure.

The company's pre-tax Weighted Average Cost of Capital (WACC) is 12%, but it is considered that an additional risk premium of 4% should be added to reflect the risk profile of this project.

(f) *Miscellaneous impairment issues*

An impairment review of the local newspaper division of Current Issues Limited took place in 2x03 with the result that the following write-downs were made in that year:

(i) Printing presses which had originally cost €400,000 were five years old on 31 December 2x03, when they were written down on 31 December 2x03 to their recoverable amount of €60,000.

Up to 2x04 the printing presses had been depreciated at 10% per annum on a straight line basis. Depreciation in 2x04 was charged on a straight line basis over the assets' remaining life of 5 years.

A positive change in consumer preferences during 2x05 has meant that the reasons which led to the original impairment have now been reversed.

(ii) Land which had been purchased in 2x00 for €300,000 was revalued to €500,000 in 2x02. As part of the impairment review it was written down on 31 December 2x03 to its recoverable amount of €200,000.

The write-down was recorded as follows:

| | DR | CR |
	€	€
Revaluation surplus – SOCI OCI	200,000	
Impairment write-down		
– SOCI P/L	100,000	
Land		300,000

Due to a revision of consumer preferences in 2x05, it is believed that there are grounds for reversing the original impairment.

(iii)   *Titles*

As part of the 2x03 impairment review, the book value of purchased local newspaper titles had been written down by €250,000. In retrospect this appears to have been unnecessary, following improvements in content which have resulted in more positive findings on consumer preferences in 2x05.

(g)   *Miscellaneous provisions and contingency issues*

(i)   Legal action

On 30 November 2x05 a well known celebrity took a libel action against Current Issues Limited. The case is due to come before the courts in June 2x06, and the plaintiff has refused to accept an unconditional apology, together with a cash settlement of €80,000.

On 31 March 2x06 (the date on which the directors of Current Issues authorised the accounts for issue), the company's legal advisers were of the opinion that there was a 75% probability that the plaintiff would be awarded damages of €100,000. Additionally, they estimated that there was a 25% probability that damages as high as €200,000 could be awarded.

Current Issues have sought to recover part of the award from a publicity group which allegedly leaked false information about the celebrity. On 31 March 2x06 it seemed probable that a cash settlement of €20,000 might be agreed.

(ii)   Review of provisions

In finalising the 2x05 accounts, the Board of Directors of Current Issues Limited is carrying out a review of provisions:

- A decision to restructure a division within Current Issues Limited was taken at a board meeting in December 2x04, and a provision of €250,000 was made at that time. An outline plan for the restructuring was finalised in December 2x05.

- A provision for the ongoing repair of printing presses was increased by 20% to €300,000 during 2x05. It is expected that a significant proportion of this provision will be required during 2x06.

- At 31 December 2x05, the present value of future un-provided decommissioning expenses of existing printing presses was estimated at €300,000.

(iii) Payments to retired employees

Due to legislative changes in 2x05, Current Issues Limited has been forced to agree to make additional pension payments to retired employees. The additional amounts which will be payable are as follows:

	€
2x06	150,000
2x07	200,000
2x08	250,000
2x09	280,000
2x10	320,000
2x11	350,000

(h) *Tangible Non-Current Assets*

(i) Capitalisation of costs

During 2x05 Current Issues decided to construct a specialised mini-printing press for the production of advertising leaflets which were to be circulated as newspaper inserts. The following costs were incurred during 2x05:

	€
Purchase of machine part components (before deducting trade discount of 5%)	20,000
Option premium to guarantee availability of external labour personnel paid in January 2x05*	3,000
External labour costs	10,000
Labour costs of own employees	13,000
Safety and clearance check procedures	2,000
Correction of design errors	3,000

Marketing costs associated with advertising leaflets	
- incurred during construction	1,000
- incurred after completion of construction	1,000
Trial print runs	2,000
Interest costs	3,000
Estimated present value cost @ 31/12/2x05 of dismantling mini-printing press	1,500
	59,500

*This option premium was paid when it was probable that construction of the mini-printing press would proceed.

At 31 December 2x05, it was apparent that the proposal to produce the advertising inserts was not going to be as profitable as was first thought. At this point it was estimated that the printing press had the following values:

• Net selling price €40,000.
• Value in use €42,000.

Printing presses are depreciated at 10% on a straight line basis. A full year's depreciation is provided in the year of purchase/production. The residual value of the mini-printing press is estimated at €5,000 (€7,000 based on future prices).

(ii) Subsequent expenditure
The following items have been capitalised by Current Issues Limited in the year ended 31 December 2x05:

• Costs of the annual overhaul of the company's printing presses, amounting to €200,000.
• Removal of partitioning in factory costing €100,000, so as to increase worker productivity.
• Replacement of lifts in the company headquarters, costing €200,000. The original lifts were depreciated at 10% per annum on a reducing balance basis. The office headquarters building is depreciated at 2% per annum on a straight line basis.
• Relocation costs of printing presses amounting to €30,000.
• Extension of warehouse, costing €120,000.

(iii) Revaluation gains

    (a) Current Issues Limited purchased an office building in 2x02 for €1 million. The building has been used by the company staff, and has been depreciated at 2% per annum on a straight line basis. On 31 December 2x05 an external valuer has estimated the fair value of the property to be €1.5 million.

    (b) Current Issues purchased a factory building in 2x03 for €500,000. The building was being depreciated on a straight line basis over a useful life of 50 years with zero residual value. On 31 December 2x04 the building was revalued to €300,000, and was further revalued to €490,000 on 31 December 2x05.

(iv) Revaluation losses

    (I) Current Issues Limited purchased a site in 2x02 for €400,000, which was intended to be used for the construction of a paper storage warehouse. In 2x05 it was decided not to proceed with the construction of the warehouse. The market value of the site at 31 December 2x05 is estimated at €300,000.

    (II) At 31 December 2x04 a property which had been purchased by Current Issues Limited in 2x03 for €750,000 was revalued to €1 million. Due to a general fall in property values, the fair value of the property at 31 December 2x05 was estimated at €600,000. The property was depreciated on a straight line basis over 50 years with zero residual value.

(v) Disposals

During 2x05, Current Issues Limited disposed of land which had cost €200,000 in 2x02, and had subsequently been revalued to €310,000 during 2x04. The net proceeds of disposal amounted to €370,000.

(i) Accounting Policy Issues

(i) Research and development

At 31 December 2x04, Current Issues had €2 million of development costs included under intangible assets in the Statement of Financial Position. Previously, development costs had been written off in accordance with the expected sales revenue of future periods. The Directors have decided however that, commencing in 2x05, development costs should be written off by reference to the expected time horizon of future sales, as new information indicates that this would better reflect the consumption of the future economic benefits of the development expenditure.

(ii)   Investment Property
Current Issues Limited purchased a freehold premises in 2x03 for €3 million. The premises, which was used by company personnel, was included in the financial statements at cost, and was not depreciated.

In December 2x05, the premises was no longer used by company personnel, and it was let to an unrelated party at a market rental. The premises is included in the financial statements at 31 December 2x05 at its fair value of €5 million.

(j)   *Profit before taxation*
The profit before taxation of the Current Issues Group for the year ended 31 December 2x05 amounted to €850,000.

Requirement:

You are required to write a report to the Finance Director of the Current Issues Group, outlining how the above transactions should be accounted for in the consolidated financial statements and, where appropriate, in the financial statements of the individual companies in the group.
(Ignore tax)

The Current Issues Group has a weighted average cost of capital of 8%. This equates to 12% on a pre-tax basis.

The structure of the Current Issues Group is outlined in Appendix I.

Appendix I – Group Structure

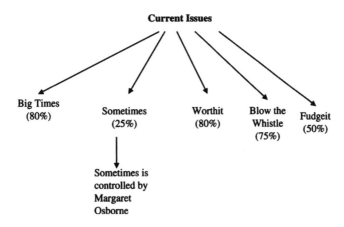

Other Companies:

(1) **Fine Tune** – owned by Margaret Osborne's husband

(2) **Money Limited** – A wholly-owned subsidiary of a merchant bank Money Limited owns the other 50% of Fudgeit

(3) **No Time Limited** – No relationship with Current Issues Group

FRONTPAGE GROUP

Introduction

You are an audit senior in a firm of Chartered Accountants, Rockwell, Spate & Co. It is February 2x06 and you are currently reviewing the draft financial statements of the Frontpage Group which has recently become a client of your firm.

Frontpage Limited is a publishing company which was set up by John Walker. In 2x00 Frontpage Limited acquired 100% of the equity share capital of Backpage Limited.

In 2x02 Frontpage Limited purchased 30% of Sideissue Limited for €5 million. John Walker had been a director of Sideissue Limited since 2x02, but resigned from the Board on the disposal of Frontpage Limited's interest in Sideissue for €9 million on the 30 September 2x05. Sideissue had been included in the group accounts using the equity method of accounting.

A number of accounting issues have arisen in respect of the audit of the Frontpage Group for the year ended 31 December 2x05. The audit manager, Patrick Queally, has requested that you review these issues and send him a memorandum. Your report should set out the appropriate accounting treatment and disclosure in respect of each accounting issue, together with any necessary associated journal adjustments.

The accounting issues and the draft financial statements are set out in Appendix I and II respectively.

Requirement

Based on the accounting issues given in Appendix I, and the draft financial statements in Appendix II, prepare a memorandum to the audit manager of Rockwell Spate & Co. in which you undertake the following:

Set out your advice in relation to the accounting treatment, together with any journal adjustments and disclosures required in respect of each of the following accounting issues arising during the 2x05 audit:

(1)	Inventory	**11 marks**
(2)	Financing arrangement	**4 marks**
(3)	Disposal of shares in Sideissue Limited, and related issues	**10 marks**
(4)	Construction of office building	**9 marks**
(5)	Legal and miscellaneous issues	**8 marks**
(6)	Deferred tax	**8 marks**
		Total 50 marks

including their impact, if any, on:

   (i)   the separate/individual financial statements of the respective companies;
  (ii)   the consolidated financial statements of the Frontpage Group.

Notes:

   (i)   **Re-drafted financial statements are NOT required. However, your report should include the journal entries in respect of any accounting adjustments required in respect of each accounting issue.**

  (ii)   **The Frontpage Group currently pays corporation tax at 25%, but it is possible that this rate will increase to 40% in 2x06. Capital gains tax is levied on chargeable gains at 20%.**

 (iii)   **In its separate financial statements, Frontpage Limited accounts at cost for investments in subsidiaries, joint ventures and associates.**

Appendix I

Accounting issues arising in respect of the 2x05 Financial Statements

(1) Inventory in Frontpage Limited

(i) *Publishing delay*

Work on a history book had been scheduled for completion in December 2x05. It has been discovered, however, that a series of illustrations which had been photographed on location have been misplaced. These were re-taken in January 2x06, and the book will now be published in April 2x06. It had been hoped to publish before a rival publication from Associated History Books Ltd, but it is unlikely that this will now be achieved. Consequently, sales are expected to be only 60% of the budgeted sales level of €750,000.

Costs incurred at 31 December 2x05, which have been included in inventory, are as follows:

	€'000
Materials	100
Production salaries*	150
Depreciation of equipment	20
General administration	40
Selling and distribution costs	80
	390

*Includes €30,000 in respect of misplaced book illustrations.

Further costs are estimated as follows, of which 50% have already been incurred in January/February 2x06:

	€'000
Production salaries**	90
Selling and distribution costs	220
	310

**Includes €40,000 in respect of book illustrations

(ii)   *Printing stationery*

In previous years Frontpage had outsourced its printing needs, but printing has been performed in-house since 1 January 2x05.

15,000 reams of printing stationery are included in inventory at 31 December 2x05. This inventory is held in a sealed warehouse, and additional reams of paper are stored on top of existing reams. During 2x05 five consignments of printing stationery were received, each containing 10,000 reams. The cost per ream of the first consignment was €11.40 (net of a trade discount of 5%), and this increased by 5% for each of the other four consignment lots received. Stationery inventory has been included in the financial statements on a last-in first-out basis at 31 December 2x05.

During 2x05, the inventory of stationery did not fall below 10,000 reams at any time. After the second consignment was received, the level of stationery inventory did not fall below 15,000 reams. Inventories of stationery have been included in the financial statements at 31 December 2x05 on a LIFO basis.

(iii)   *Excess dye*

Frontpage Limited's production process gives rise to a dye residue, which is sold to a nearby furniture manufacturer. Frontpage had inventories of dye with a net realisable value of €50,000 on hand at the 31 December 2x05. This has resulted from two months of printing production.

No record of the inventories of dye has been made in the financial statements at 31 December 2x05.

(2)   Financing arrangement

The trade receivables of €10.3 million were factored by Frontpage Limited in December 2x05. The factor provided an immediate advance of €8 million. The balance of €2.3 million will continue to accrue to Frontpage Limited.

The funds were advanced by the factor on the following basis:

In respect of the trade receivables of €10.3m Frontpage Limited is liable for the first €3.3m of bad debts.

All of the funds advanced by the factor were included as a current liability in the financial statements of Frontpage Limited at 31 December 2x05.

A bad debts provision of 5% of gross debtors should be provided for at 31 December 2x05. A provision of €250,000 was included in the Statement of Financial Position at 31 December 2x04.

In January 2x06 one of the company's best customers unexpectedly went into liquidation. The balance on that debtor's account at 31 December 2x05 amounted to €500,000. No adjustment has been made to the financial statements in respect of the customer's liquidation.

(3) Disposal of shares in Sideissue Limited, and related issues

(i) Sideissue had retained earnings of €4 million when Frontpage acquired its interest in 2x02. On 31 December 2x04, the retained earnings of Sideissue had increased to €7 million.

Sideissue earned profit before taxation of €2 million in the nine months ending 30 September 2x05, and incurred taxation of €600,000 on these profits.

(ii) In the nine months ending 30 September 2x05, Backpage Limited recorded sales of €900,000 to Sideissue at cost plus 10%. Backpage normally earns a mark-up of 50% on sales. None of these goods are included in the inventory of Sideissue at 30 September 2x05.

(iii) Sideissue was included in the Group Financial Statements using the equity method of accounting.

(4) Construction of office building

On 1 January 2x03 Backpage Limited commenced the construction of a new office building, and the building was completed on 30 November 2x03. It was discovered however that planning laws had been contravened, and it was not possible to occupy the offices due to a restraining order imposed by the Council. Costs of €1 million had been incurred and these were written off in full in Backpage Limited's 2x03 financial statements.

On 1 March 2x05 planning permission was granted retrospectively and the costs previously written off were reinstated, and credited to profit or loss by Backpage Limited.

Backpage depreciates buildings at 2% per annum on a straight line basis. A full year's depreciation is charged in the year of purchase or construction, and no depreciation is charged in the year of disposal. Depreciation has been charged for the year ended 31 December 2x05.

In December 2x05 the Board capitalised €300,000 of interest costs as part of buildings. These costs were incurred in respect of the financing of the new office building for the following periods:

	€'000
1 January 2x03 – 30 November 2x03	100
1 December 2x03 – 1 March 2x05	200
	300

(5) Legal and miscellaneous issues

(i)   In November 2x05 another publishing group threatened to take legal action against Frontpage, claiming breach of copyright. In a phone call to John Walker, the company's marketing director accused Frontpage of infringing their exclusive rights to publish a Brazilian musician's collected works, and threatened to sue for sales rights amounting to €0.5 million. In mid-February 2x06, no further action had been taken, and John Walker has dismissed the claim as ludicrous, maintaining that Frontpage would be able to lodge a counter-claim for copyright infringement against the same company for a similar amount.

(ii) In December 2x05 a local art expert maintained that a painting in Frontpage Limited's headquarters was worth in the region of €700,000. On 10 January 2x06, while still awaiting confirmation of its value, the painting was sold for €350,000 to Margin Limited, a company in which John Walker's son, Thomas, had a controlling interest.

On 21 January 2x06 the value of the painting was confirmed at €700,000. The painting had been purchased for €10,000 several years ago and, at 31 December 2x05, it is included in property, plant and equipment at its net book value of €8,000.

(6) **Deferred Tax**

General issues

At 31 December 2x05, the following issues arose in respect of Frontpage Limited:

(i) The net book value of plant and machinery at 31 December 2x05 was €1.4 million. The tax written down value of this plant and machinery amounted to €900,000 at the same date.

(ii) Pension costs of €300,000 were accrued at 31 December 2x05, and deposit interest included as a prepayment amounted to €80,000. It should be assumed that pension costs are allowed for tax purposes when paid, and that deposit interest is taxed on a cash receipts basis.

(iii) There was a revaluation surplus of €500,000 in respect of land at 31 December 2x05. It is intended to retain the land within the group for the foreseeable future.

(iv) Development costs capitalised at 31 December 2x05 amount to €250,000, all of which has been paid and fully claimed for tax purposes. Frontpage Limited writes off development costs at 20% per annum, on a straight line basis.

(v) Frontpage Limited had made a provision for deferred taxation of €100,000 at 31 December 2x04, and this provision was unchanged at 31 December 2x05. None of the provision at 31 December 2x04 related to the revaluation of land referred to in (iii) above.

Appendix II

Draft Statement of Comprehensive Income of the Frontpage Group for the year ended 31 December 2x05

	€'000
Revenue	14,500
Cost of sales	(6,900)
Gross profit	7,600
Distribution costs	(400)
Administrative expenses	(700)
Other expenses	(3,500)
Share of profit of associate	600
Profit on disposal of Sideissue Ltd	4,000
Finance costs	(600)
Profit before tax	7,000
Income tax expense	(750)
Profit for the year from continuing operations	6,250

Other comprehensive income:
Items that may subsequently be reclassified to profit or loss:

Share of other comprehensive income of associate	250
Cash flow hedges	750
Total comprehensive income for the year	7,250

Profit attributable to:

Owners of the parent	6,250
Non-controlling interests	–
	6,250

Total comprehensive income attributable to:

Owners of the parent	7,250
Non-controlling interests	–
	7,250

Draft Statement of Financial Position of the Frontpage Group at 31 December 2x05

	Notes	€'000
Assets		
Non-current assets		
Property, plant and equipment		15,500
Current assets		
Inventories		1,500
Trade and other receivables		10,900*
Cash and cash equivalents		700
		13,100
Total assets		28,600
Liabilities		
Current liabilities		
Trade and other payables		14,200
Income tax payable		1,600
		15,800
Non-current liabilities		
Term loan		1,200
Deferred income taxes		100
		1,300
Total liabilities		17,100
Net assets		11,500
Equity		
Equity attributable to owners of the parent		
Share capital		1,000
Share premium account		3,000
Revaluation surplus		1,500
Retained earnings		6,000
Total equity		11,500

*Includes trade receivables of €10.3 million

HARDCOURT GROUP

Introduction

You are an audit senior in a firm of Chartered Accountants, Comerford Lane & Co. It is February 2x06 and you are currently reviewing the draft financial statements of the Hardcourt Group which has recently become a client of your firm.

The Hardcourt Group consists of Hardcourt Limited and its subsidiary company, Claycourt Limited, which was acquired during 2x05. The Group's principal area of business is focused on the sales of timber products and ancillary activities. A number of accounting issues have arisen in respect of the audit of the Hardcourt Group for the year ended 31 December 2x05. The audit manager, Beatrice Lambe, has requested that you review these issues and send her a memorandum. Your report should set out the appropriate accounting treatment and disclosure in respect of each accounting issue, together with any necessary associated journal adjustments.

The accounting issues and the draft financial statements are set out in Appendix I and II respectively.

Requirement:

Based on the accounting issues outlined in Appendix I, and the draft financial statements in Appendix II, prepare a memorandum to the audit manager of Comerford Lane & Co. in which you undertake the following:

Set out your advice in relation to the accounting treatment, together with any journal adjustments and disclosures required in respect of each of the following accounting issues arising during the 2x05 audit:

(1)	Acquisition of Claycourt Limited	**20 marks**
(2)	Revaluation of land	**4 marks**
(3)	Restructuring	**10 marks**
(4)	Land	**4 marks**
(5)	Capital grants	**7 marks**
(6)	Financing arrangement	**5 marks**

Total 50 marks

including their impact, if any, on:

    (i)   the separate/individual financial statements of the respective companies;

    (ii) the consolidated financial statements of the Hardcourt Group.

Notes:

    (i)   **Re-drafted financial statements are NOT required. However, your report should include the journal entries in respect of any accounting adjustments required in respect of each accounting issue.**

    (ii) **The Hardcourt Group pays capital gains tax @ 20%. The corporation tax rate is 30%.**

    (iii) **It is group policy to measure non-controlling interests at acquisition date at their proportionate share of the identifiable net assets of a subsidiary.**

Appendix I

Accounting issues arising in respect of the 2x05 Financial Statements of the Hardcourt Group

(1) Acquisition of Claycourt Limited

On 1 July 2x05, Hardcourt Limited acquired 85% of the ordinary share capital of Claycourt Limited for €8.5 million in cash. The book value of the identifiable net assets of Claycourt Limited at that time was €7 million. The following details are relevant to the acquisition:

- It has since transpired that work in progress inventory of Claycourt, which had a book value of €500,000 on 1 July 2x05, was subsequently sold for €400,000. Completion costs amounted to €70,000.
- The costs of a due diligence investigation of Claycourt Limited amounted to €400,000. This was written off to the Statement of Comprehensive Income of Hardcourt Limited.
- Quoted investments with a book value of €300,000, held as current assets by Claycourt Limited, had a market value of €800,000.
- Sales of timber products by Claycourt Limited to Hardcourt Limited amounted to €200,000 per calendar month during 2x05. Hardcourt Limited had one month's inventory on hand at 31 December 2x05, which had been acquired from Claycourt Limited at a mark-up of 25% on cost.

No entries, other than the write-off of due diligence costs, have been made in respect of the acquisition of Claycourt Limited.

(2) Revaluation of Land

Land purchased by Hardcourt Limited in 2x03 for €1 million had been revalued to €1.5 million in 2x04. A rezoning decision in 2x05 has reduced the value of the land to €700,000 at 31 December 2x05.

(3) Restructuring

During 2x05 a detailed restructuring plan for Hardcourt Limited was drawn up, involving the closure of the timberland division, details of which were announced to the staff in October. Operating activities, however, cannot cease until 31 May 2x06 due to contractual commitments with customers. It is estimated that operating losses during the first five months of 2x06 will amount to €600,000. It is intended to dispose of all of the saleable assets of the division as part of a single transaction.

It is expected that the following additional costs will be incurred:

Redundancy costs
Redundancy costs are expected to amount in total to €1 million. It is believed, however, that there is a 60% probability of re-deploying some staff, which would result in €200,000 of the redundancy costs being avoided.

(4) Land

A land site owned by Hardcourt Limited is surplus to requirements and, in December 2x05, the site was put on sale at an amount which is €300,000 more than its value in the Statement of Financial Position at 31 December 2x05. It is expected that the site will be sold for this amount during 2x06.

The land had been purchased several years ago for €800,000, and is valued in the financial statements at 31 December 2x05 at €1.7 million. Selling costs are estimated at €30,000.

(5) Capital grants

Hardcourt Limited has always recorded amounts of grants received on a cash receipts basis. The Board of Directors has now decided that grants should be recorded in the financial statements when Government commitments are in place. This decision has been taken on the grounds that an accruals basis will provide information that is reliable and more relevant.

At 31 December 2x05 Hardcourt Limited had received commitments for grants of 25% in respect of machinery costing €800,000 purchased during November and December.

One of the machines was transferred to Claycourt Limited at its cost price of €200,000 soon after the date of purchase.

Appendix II

Draft Statement of Comprehensive Income of the Hardcourt Group for the year ended 31 December 2x05

	2x05 €'000
Revenue	17,900
Cost of sales	(5,850)
Gross profit	12,050
Distribution costs	(700)
Administrative expenses	(600)
Other expenses	(2,100)
Finance costs	(620)
Profit before tax	8,030
Income tax expense	(750)
Profit for the year from continuing operations	7,280
Other comprehensive income:	
Items that will not be reclassified to profit or loss:	
Gains on property revaluation	1,230
Items that may be subsequently reclassified to profit or loss:	
Cash flow hedges	750
Total comprehensive income for the year	9,260
Profit attributable to:	
Owners of the parent	6,450
Non-controlling interests	830
	7,280
Total comprehensive income attributable to:	
Owners of the parent	8,430
Non-controlling interests	830
	9,260

Draft Statement of Financial Position of the Hardcourt Group at 31 December 2x05

	Notes	2x05 €'000	2x04 €'000
Assets			
Non-current assets			
Property, plant and equipment		20,943	
Current assets			
Inventories		4,469	
Trade and other receivables		5,395	
Cash and cash equivalents		1,155	
		11,01	
Total assets		31,962	
Liabilities			
Current liabilities			
Trade and other payables		3,565	
Non-current liabilities			
Term loan		1,120	
Total liabilities		4,685	
Net assets		27,277	
Equity			
Equity attributable to owners of the parent			
Share capital		100	
Share premium account		5,250	
Revaluation surplus		7,500	
Retained earnings		12,927	
		25,777	
Non-controlling interests		1,500	
Total equity		27,277	

HEALTHFIRST GROUP

Introduction

You are an audit senior in a firm of Chartered Accountants, Lantry Mansfield & Co. It is February 2x06 and you are currently reviewing the draft financial statements of the Healthfirst Group which has recently become a client of your firm.

Healthfirst Limited is a medical goods company which was set up by Edward Smithson some years ago. Healthfirst Limited has a number of subsidiaries, which include an 85% shareholding in Scanright Limited, acquired on 1 April 2x05, with a view to diversifying into a growth area in the diagnostic goods sector. All other subsidiaries are 100% owned by Healthfirst Limited.

A number of accounting issues have arisen in respect of the audit of the Healthfirst Group for the year ended 31 December 2x05. The audit manager, Susan Gilmartin, has requested that you review these issues and send her a memorandum. Your memorandum should set out the appropriate accounting treatment and disclosure in respect of each accounting issue, together with any necessary associated journal adjustments.

The accounting issues and the draft financial statements are set out in Appendix I and II respectively.

Requirement:

Based on the accounting issues outlined in Appendix I, and the draft financial statements in Appendix II, prepare a memorandum to the audit manager of Lantry Mansfield & Co. in which you undertake the following:

Set out your advice in relation to the accounting treatment, together with any journal adjustments and disclosures required in respect, of each of the following accounting issues arising during the 2x05 audit:

(1)	Goodwill on the acquisition of Scanright Limited, and relevant disclosures	**10 marks**
(2)	Inter-company sales	**9 marks**
(3)	Deferred tax	**13 marks**
(4)	Investment property	**8 marks**
(5)	Sale of franchise	**10 marks**
		Total 50 marks

including their impact, if any, on:

    (i)   the separate and individual financial statements of the respective companies;

    (ii) the consolidated financial statements of the Healthfirst Group.

Notes:

- **Re-drafted financial statements are NOT required. However, your report should include the journal entries in respect of any accounting adjustments required in respect of each accounting issue.**
- **The Healthfirst Group currently pays corporation tax at 25%, but it is possible that this rate will increase to 40% in 2x05. Capital gains tax is levied on chargeable gains at 20%.**
- **In its separate financial statements, Healthfirst Limited accounts at cost for investments in subsidiaries, joint ventures and associates.**
- **It is group policy to measure any non-controlling interest in subsidiaries at acquisition date at fair value. The fair value of non-controlling interests should be computed as a proportion of the amount paid by Healthfirst for a controlling interest.**

Appendix I

Accounting issues arising in respect of the 2x05 Financial Statements

(1) Goodwill arising on acquisition of Scanright Limited

On 1 April 2x05 Healthfirst paid €6.5 million for an 85% interest in Scanright. Scanright had the following shareholders' funds at this date:

	€'000
Equity share capital	1,000
Reserves	3,800

It was estimated that the market value of Scanright's land holdings was €800,000 greater than their net book value at that time.

Finished goods included in Scanright's inventory at 1 April 2x05 have been in the company's warehouse since 31 December 2x04. They were included in the Statement of Financial Position of Scanright at their production cost of €395,000.

These goods were sold in June 2x05 for €300,000.

(2) Inter-company sales

During 2x05 Scanright sold goods evenly throughout the year to Healthfirst Limited for €960,000. Scanright charged a mark up of 25% on cost, and 20% of the goods remained in the inventory of Healthfirst at 31 December 2x05. The latter goods had been purchased from Scanright after 1 April 2x05.

(3) Deferred Tax

At 31 December 2x05, the following information is available in respect of the Healthfirst Group (excluding Scanright Limited):

(a) Land purchased in 2x00 for €1 million was revalued to €1.5 million at 31 December 2x04. An agreement was signed in November 2x05 to sell this land in March 2x06.

(b) Deposit interest of €50,000 was recorded in the financial statements of the Group at 31 December 2x05, but was not received until February of 2x06.

(c) The tax written-down value of plant and machinery at 31 December 2x05 was €1.4 million. The net book value at that date was €2 million.

(d) Development costs are allowed for taxation purposes when paid, and are expensed to the statement of comprehensive income of the Health-first Group over five years, commencing at the point of commercial production. All expenditure incurred was capitalised and has been paid for in full at 31 December 2x05.

(e) During 2x05 the Healthfirst Group incurred fines amounting to €100,000 for a breach of planning guidelines.

(f) A provision of €100,000 has been provided at 31 December 2x05 for deferred taxation. None of this provision relates to the revaluation gain on land.

(4) Investment property

An office building which was purchased in 2x01 for €700,000 was let to a third party at a market rental. This building was included in the financial statements of the Healthfirst Group as an investment property at its fair value – €1.3 million at 31 December 2x04.

On 1 January 2x05 the lease agreement terminated, and the building was used by the Healthfirst Group as a staff office. The Healthfirst Group depreciates buildings at 2% per annum on a straight line basis.

(5) Sale of franchise

In 2x01, Suretime Limited, a 100% subsidiary of Healthfirst Limited, purchased a franchise for a lifestyle drug for €1 million. This amount was capitalised and was not amortised. On 1 November 2x05 the franchise was sold by Suretime Limited to a US pharmaceutical firm for $2.5 million, the sales proceeds being included in turnover at the spot rate on that date.

On 20 December 2x05 Suretime Limited received full payment from the US purchaser of the franchise. In the expectation of a rise in the value of the dollar, the $2.5 million sales proceeds were held in a $ bank account. Following a strengthening of the dollar, the funds were converted into € on 15 February 2x06.

Exchange rates were as follows:

1 November 2x05:   €1 = $1.1
20 December 2x05:   €1 = $1.05

31 December 2x05:   €1 = $1
15 February 2x06:   €1 = $.95

Appendix II

Extract from Draft Statement of Comprehensive Income of the Healthfirst Group for the year ended 31 December 2x05

	2x05 €'000
Revenue	15,500
Cost of sales	(5,400)
Gross profit	10,100
Distribution costs	(400)
Administrative expenses	(700)
Other expenses	(1,500)
Finance costs	(600)
Share of profit of associate	600
Profit before tax	7,500
Income tax expense	(750)
Profit for the year from continuing operations	6,750
Other comprehensive income:	
Items that will not be reclassified to profit or loss:	
Gains on property revaluation	750
Items that may be subsequently reclassified to profit or loss:	
Cash flow hedges	200
Total comprehensive income for the year	7,700
Profit attributable to:	
Owners of the parent	6,450
Non-controlling interests	300
	6,750
Total comprehensive income attributable to:	
Owners of the parent	7,350
Non-controlling interests	350
	7,700

Draft Statement of Financial Position of the Healthfirst Group
at 31 December 2x05

	Notes	€'000
Assets		
Non-current assets		
Property, plant and equipment		6,000
Development costs		800
		6,800
Current assets		
Inventories		1,500
Trade and other receivables		14,000
Cash and cash equivalents		1,300
		16,800
Total Assets		23,600
Liabilities		
Current liabilities		
Trade and other payables		5,800
Non-current liabilities		
Term loan		1,200
Deferred income taxes		100
		1,300
Total liabilities		7,100
Net assets		16,500
Equity		
Equity attributable to owners of the parent		
Share capital		1,000
Share premium account		3,000
Revaluation reserve		2,100
Retained earnings		9,300
		15,400
Non-controlling Interest		1,100
Total equity		16,500

MAINPART GROUP

Introduction

You are an audit senior in a firm of Chartered Accountants, Witherspoon Holt & Co. It is February 2x06 and you are currently reviewing the draft financial statements of the Mainpart Group, which has recently become a client of your firm.

The Mainpart Group consists of Mainpart Holdings Limited and two wholly-owned subsidiary undertakings, Mainpart Limited and Rent Part Limited. The group's principal area of business is the sales of cement products and ancillary activities. A number of accounting issues have arisen in respect of the audit of the Mainpart Group for the year ended 31 December 2x05. The Senior Partner of Witherspoon Holt & Co., Judith Holt, has requested that you review these issues and prepare a report for the Board of Directors of Mainpart Holdings Limited. Your report should set out the appropriate accounting treatment and disclosure in respect of each accounting issue, together with any necessary associated journal adjustments.

The accounting issues and the draft financial statements are set out in Appendix I and II respectively. The Group structure is outlined in Appendix III.

Requirement:

Based on the accounting issues outlined in Appendix I, and the draft financial statements in Appendix II, prepare a report to the Board of Directors of Mainpart Holdings Limited in which you undertake the following:

Set out your advice in relation to the appropriate accounting treatment, together with any journal adjustments and disclosures required in respect of each of the following accounting issues arising during the 2x05 audit:

(1) Construction of Building   **20 marks**

(2) Disposal of Subsidiary   **13 marks**

(3) Restructuring   **12 marks**

(4) Disposal of Land   <u>**5 marks**</u>

Total 50 marks

including their impact, if any, on:

  (i)   the separate/individual financial statements of the respective companies; and
  (ii) the consolidated financial statements of the Mainpart Group.

NB Redrafted or consolidated financial statements are not required. The Group's weighted average cost of capital (WACC) is 12%.

In their separate financial statements, Mainpart Holdings Limited accounts at cost for investments in subsidiaries, joint ventures and associates.

Appendix I

Accounting issues arising in respect of the 2x05 Financial Statements of the Mainpart Group Companies

(1) Construction of Building

Mainpart Limited commenced the construction of a new factory premises on 1 January 2x05. The building was completed on 31 October 2x05, and the following costs were incurred and capitalised as part of the land and buildings of Mainpart Limited:

	€'000
Site preparation costs	100
External labour costs (Note 1)	700
Materials (Note 2)	1,500
Overheads:	
- production (Note 3)	400
- general management	100
Re-design cost due to planning restrictions	170
Location map and brochure sent to customers	10
Recruitment costs of security personnel who commenced work in December 2x05	20
Interest costs (from 1 January to 31 October 2x05)	300
Official opening luncheon	30
	3,330

Note 1: External labour costs
This work was carried out by Small Part Limited, a company in which Mainpart Limited has a 22% shareholding.

A two-months' delay was caused by a work stoppage in July 2x05, which increased the total labour costs by €100,000. Funds borrowed were put on temporary deposit for the stoppage period, earning interest of €12,000.

Note 2: Materials
Materials are inclusive of VAT at 10% and before deducting a trade discount of 5%.

Note 3: Production Overheads

Staff recruited for project	100
Administrative staff redeployed from other Mainpart locations	80
Salary of safety officers	140
Other variable overheads	80
	400

(2) Disposal of Subsidiary

On 1 July 2x05 Mainpart Limited sold 90% of its shares in Subpart Limited, which supplies ancillary cement products. Disposal proceeds were €32 million in cash. One hundred per cent of Subpart Limited had been acquired on 1 January 2x03 at a cost of €22 million. The assets less liabilities of Subpart Limited were included in the group's statement of financial position at €26 million on the 1 July 2x05. Goodwill of €2 million relating to the acquisition of Subpart Limited was included in the group's statement of financial position at 1 July 2x05. The fair value of the 10% stake retained was €3.5 million at 1 July 2x05.

Mainpart Limited agreed to buy directly from Subpart Limited after the disposal date, so as to continue to service the needs of a select number of its customers. Purchases from Subpart Limited for the six months ended 31 December 2x05 amounted to €1.5 million.

(3) Restructuring

During 2x05 a re-structuring plan for Mainpart Limited's gardening division was drawn up and implemented. The following costs were incurred.

	€'000
Redundancy settlements (Note 1)	800
Enhanced pensions for staff laid off (Note 2)	2,640
Provision for continuing losses expected in 2x06 and 2007	1,000
	4,440

Note 1: Redundancy settlements
These amounts were paid early in 2x06. It is likely that further redundancy costs of €300,000 will be incurred. It is believed, however, that these costs can be avoided, and that the staff can be redeployed elsewhere within the company. This would necessitate a retraining programme, which would cost in the region of €100,000.

Note 2: Enhanced pensions
It has been agreed to pay an enhanced pension to staff who have been laid off. This will cost €220,000 per annum for the next 12 years. The first annual instalment was paid by the company on 1 January 2x06.

Note 3: Other costs
A five-year lease agreement was signed on 1 January 2x05 in respect of a building which is now being vacated. The terms of the lease require the payment of annual lease instalments of €90,000, payable in advance. Mainpart Limited is confident that half of this amount can be recouped by subletting the premises to another tenant.

(4) Disposal of Land

On 28 December 2x05, land in a newly-acquired subsidiary, Rent Part Limited, was sold for €2 million to Robert Thompson, the managing director of that company. Settlement was deferred until February 2x06. The land had cost €800,000 in 2x02, and the disposal has been accounted for in accordance with IAS 16 'Property, Plant and Equipment'. On 12 January 2x06, the land was re-purchased by Rent Part Limited for €2 million.

Appendix II

Draft Financial Statements for the Year Ended 31 December 2x05

Statement of Financial Position as at 31 December 2x05

	Mainpart Holdings Limited	Mainpart Limited	Rent Part Limited
	€'000	€'000	€'000
Non-current assets			
Property, plant & equipment	300	21,000	9,200
Financial assets:			
Mainpart Limited	5,700	–	
Small Part Limited	10,000	–	–
Rent Part Limited	15,000		
	31,000	21,000	9,200
Current assets			
Inventories	–	4,400	4,500
Trade and other receivables	–	3,600	2,700
Cash and cash equivalents	–	1,900	1,100
	–	9,900	8,300
Total assets	31,000	30,900	17,500
Liabilities			
Current Liabilities			
Trade and other payables	250	4,000	2,900
Non-current liabilities			
Convertible debentures	10,000	–	–
Total liabilities	10,250	4,000	2,900
Net assets	20,750	26,900	14,600
Equity			
Share capital	17,000	1,000	1,000
Revaluation surplus	–	1,460	–
Retained earnings	3,750	24,440	13,600
Total equity	20,750	26,900	14,600

Statements of Comprehensive Income for the Year Ended 31 December 2x05

	Mainpart Holdings Limited	Mainpart Limited	Rent Part Limited
	€'000	€'000	€'000
Revenue	–	28,000	22,000
Cost of Sales	–	(16,000)	(12,000)
Gross profit	–	12,000	10,000
Other income	3000	–	–
Distribution costs	–	(1,500)	
Administrative expenses	(800)	(2,000)	(3500)
Other expenses	–	(500)	
Finance Costs	(1500)	(1,000)	(700)
Profit on disposal of land	–	–	1,200
Profit on sale of Subpart Ltd	–	10,000	–
Profit before tax	700	17,000	7,000
Income tax expense	(350)	(4,500)	(2,600)
Profit for the year from continuing operations	350	12,500	4,400
Other comprehensive income: Items that will not be reclassified to profit or loss:			
Gains on property revaluation	–	340	–
Total comprehensive income for the year	350	12,840	4,400

Appendix III

Group Structure

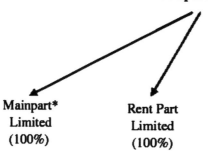

Mainpart Holdings Limited

Mainpart*
Limited
(100%)

Rent Part
Limited
(100%)

*Mainpart Limited held a 100% interest in Subpart Limited until 1 July 2x05. On that date it disposed of 90% of its shareholding in Subpart.

MILLENNIUM GROUP

The Millennium Group has a substantial presence in the technology field. The Group comprises Millennium Plc and a number of wholly-owned subsidiary companies which have been acquired over a number of years. The draft consolidated financial statements of the Group for the year ended 31 December 2x05 are set out in Appendix I. As the newly appointed Financial Accountant of the Group, you are reviewing the draft financial statements, and the following matters have come to your attention:

(1) Sale of Land

On 1 December 2x05, Millennium Plc has agreed to sell a block of land for €1,500,000 which had cost €1,000,000 in 2x01. Consideration for the purchase is being deferred until 1 July 2x06, to allow time for the purchaser, a newly established building firm, to apply for planning permission for the construction of a housing development.

The land had been revalued to €1,200,000 at 31 December 2x04 in the consolidated financial statements of the Millennium Group. The sale has been recorded by Millennium Plc and the deferred consideration has been included in debtors.

(2) Depreciation of Building

On 1 January 2x05, a subsidiary of Millennium Plc, Century Limited, purchased a building for €1,600,000. The building has an estimated useful life of 50 years, but it is expected that it will be sold by the Group in 10 years' time.

The estimated residual value in 10 years' time, based on 2x05 prices, is €1,500,000 (€2 million including expected inflation). On the basis that the expected residual value exceeds the cost of the building, Century Limited has not charged depreciation on the asset for the year ended 31 December 2x05.

(3) Sale of Subsidiary

On 1 July 2x05 Millennium Plc sold a wholly-owned subsidiary, Leading Edge Limited. Up to the time of its disposal, Leading Edge Limited had contributed 50% of the Group's data backup sales. The remaining customers in this sector will still continue to be fully serviced by the other companies in the Group.

Leading Edge Limited had turnover of €3 million, and operating profit of €1 million for the six months ended 30 June 2x05, and its results have been included in the draft consolidated financial statements in accordance with IFRS 3 *Business Combinations.*

(4) Software Costs

During 2x05 a number of issues have arisen in respect of software costs. All of the costs incurred have been included under intangible assets in the consolidated Statement of Financial Position of the Group, and no amounts have been amortised to date:

(a) *Externally purchased software*

During the year, Millennium Plc purchased a variety of software to assist the operation of the Group's inventory control packages for internal purposes. The total cost amounted to €800,000, and the software on average is expected to have a useful life of five years.

However, one package included in the above total cost €100,000, and was acquired specifically to run the Group's mainframe computer, which is due to be replaced in January 2x08. It is expected that the existing software will not be compatible with the new mainframe.

The Group depreciates non-current assets on a straight-line basis over their expected useful lives, charging a full year's depreciation in the year of purchase, and charging no depreciation in the year of disposal.

(b) Software Development

A number of additional programmers were employed during 2x05 to develop software for the Group's own use. Costs incurred up to 31 December 2x05 amounted to €500,000, and the new software is due to become operational in the second half of 2x06. The costs incurred were included as an intangible asset in the financial statements.

(c) Software acquired for Development Work

Software costs of €400,000 were incurred in 2x05 to assist in the development of a new product costing system which the Group intends to market in 2x06. Initial market research had proved very promising, and the product is on course to deliver fully on its potential. Other costs associated with this project have been capitalised as development costs. The software costs of €400,000 have been expensed to the statement of comprehensive income.

(5) Investment in Future Developments Limited

- On 1 April 2x05, Millennium Plc purchased Future Developments Limited in partnership with Twentieth Century Limited, which is not related in any way to the Millennium Group. Both companies have agreed to manage the entity jointly, and the contract of agreement stipulates that the new entity is intended for long-term development. Both Millennium Plc and Twentieth Century Limited own 50% of the equity share capital of Future Developments Limited.

- The fair value of the identifiable net assets of Future Developments Limited at 1 April 2x05 was €500,000 in excess of their book value (this excess fair value has *not* subsequently been reflected in the financial statements). The book value of net assets at 1 April 2x05 was €4,883,000, and retained earnings at the same date were €3,533,000.

- On 1 July 2x05, Future Developments Limited sold a block of land (which had cost €300,000) to Millennium Plc for €600,000. It should be assumed that this gain will not incur a tax charge.

- On 1 October 2x05, Century Limited (a wholly-owned subsidiary of Millennium Plc) sold a large quantity of inventory to Future Developments Limited for €1 million. The cost of the goods to Century

Limited had been €750,000. The inventory is still held by Future Developments at 31 December 2x05.

- The draft financial statements of Future Developments for the year ended 31 December 2x05 are included in Appendix I.

Requirement:

(a) Explain what adjustments should be made to the draft financial statements of the Group in respect of the above transactions, so as to comply with recommended accounting practice.

(35 marks)

(b) Document the journal entries which will be necessary to effect the changes outlined in (a) above.

(15 marks)

Notes:

    (i) **It should be assumed that any adjustments to the draft financial statements will have no tax implications.**

    (ii) **The Group Structure is outlined in Appendix II.**

Appendix I

Draft Statement of Comprehensive Income for the Year Ended 31 December 2x05

	Millennium Group €'000	Future Dev. Limited €'000
Revenue	16,800	4,300
Cost of sales	(7,950)	(2,780)
Gross profit	8,850	1,520
Distribution costs	(600)	(100)
Administrative expenses	(420)	(80)
Other expenses	(280)	(30)
Finance costs	(620)	(418)
Profit on disposal of subsidiary	800	–
Profit on disposal of land	300	300
Profit before tax	8,030	1,192
Income tax expense	(750)	(206)
Profit for the year from continuing operations	7,280	986
Profit attributable to:		
Owners of the parent	7,280	
Non-controlling interests	–	
	7,280	

Draft Statement of Financial Position as at 31 December 2x05

	Millennium Group €'000	Future Dev. Limited €'000
Non-current assets		
Property, plant and equipment	12,943	6,105
Intangible assets	4,000	–
Investment in joint venture at cost	4,000	–
	20,943	6,105
Current assets		
Inventories	4,469	1,240
Trade and other receivables	5,395	972
Cash and cash equivalents	1,155	1,130
	11,019	3,342
Total assets	31,962	9,447
Liabilities		
Current Liabilities		
Trade and other payables	3,565	2,715
Non-current liabilities		
Term loan	1,120	1,035
Convertible debentures	2,000	–
	3,120	1,035
Total liabilities	6,685	3,750
Net assets	25,277	5,697
Equity		
Share capital	100	100
Share premium	3,250	250
Revaluation surplus	9,000	1,000
Retained earnings	12,927	4,347
Total equity	25,277	5,697

Appendix II – Group Structure

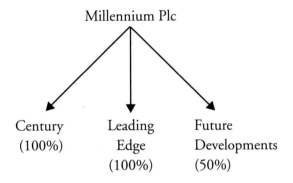

Millennium Plc

Century
(100%)

Leading
Edge
(100%)

Future
Developments
(50%)

Other companies:

Twentieth Century Limited – Millennium's joint venture partner in Future Developments.

NORMAN EPSTOW LIMITED

Introduction

Several years ago, Norman Epstow realised a childhood ambition when he founded a toy soldier factory in Galway. As a child he had been fascinated by these miniature men of war, and much of his youth was spent supervising enormous battles full of surprise attacks and tactical manoeuvres. At the age of eighteen Norman registered as a Commerce student in University College Galway. He graduated with an honours degree, and found employment as a trainee chartered accountant. Although quite adept at all aspects of his work, Norman did not find a sense of fulfilment, and he left his Firm before sitting his final examination. Having worked in a variety of jobs, Norman accumulated a modest amount of savings, and it was a chance meeting with an old friend, Stewart Dunston, that gave him the idea for his new venture. As Norman and Stewart discussed childhood memories, attention inevitably focused on Norman's fascination with toy soldiers. Stewart recalled a trip to a toy soldier factory in Birmingham the previous year, and as he described his visit, Norman had already begun to consider the potential for a business idea.

After several months spent assessing the viability of a toy soldier enterprise, Norman set up in business, operating at first from his family home. Initially it seemed that he would be unable to survive, but his dogged commitment to the business bought him some time, and the liquidation of a rival firm was to provide a lifeline. Eventually, Norman Epstow Limited acquired a new premises, and a skilled and dedicated workforce provided the inspiration for continued growth.

The most significant change in the Company's business since incorporation had been the necessity to expand the product range. The toy soldier market had been on a declining trend for some time, and the Company had diversified into the manufacture and distribution of giftware and 'classic miniatures'. This latter product was a miniature reproduction of characters from the classics of authors such as Charles Dickens. The manufacturing process required the development of master moulds, into which liquid lead is poured, which hardens to produce the desired miniature. These moulds can then be painted to make the figures appear more attractive. The development of 'master moulds' was an expensive investment, but the focus on classics provided a long shelf life for the Company's products.

Over the years Norman Epstow Limited had developed a large mail order business, with orders being received from up to 20 countries. There have been two main categories of sales:

• *Kit sales*
  This comprises the sale of miniature moulds, together with a solid block of the lead-based compound. Customers would use the kits to make their own figures which they could then paint if desired.

• *Item sales*
  This involves the in-house manufacture of completed products, encompassing the giftware and miniature range. Customers would be presented with a finished product, which had been moulded and painted by the Company's employees.

  Children comprise 80% of the kit sales market, the remaining 20% being sold to adults with a particular interest in hobby casting. Item sales are primarily an adult market.

  Norman Epstow Limited has never employed a qualified accountant to operate its accounting systems, or to prepare its annual financial statements. However, Norman himself has always kept an eye on this side of the business, and he has been involved in preparing the draft accounts for the year ended 31 December 2x05, which are attached in Appendix I.

  As audit manager for Compston & Co. Chartered Accountants you are reviewing the draft accounts, and your attention has been drawn to the following matters by I. Ambright who has worked as a senior on the job:

  (i) *Termination of toy soldier item sales*
       In April 2x05, Norman Epstow decided to terminate the production of toy soldier item sales, and to sell off assets being used for this purpose. This decision was based on declining sales, and the fact that the

product was labour intensive and earning a lower margin than other products in the item sales range. This decision was put into effect by 30 June 2x05, when all uncompleted mail order sales had been filled. For public relations, and Company image purposes, however, the toy soldier range would remain in the Company's catalogue, and occasionally an individual piece would be supplied to one of the Company's most important customers. For this reason, Norman Epstow regarded toy soldier item sales as an ongoing activity.

Toy soldier item sales comprised 40% of the value of total item sales in 2x01, but declined at the rate of 25% per annum in each subsequent year. Toy soldier item sales have had a gross margin of 15% for several years, and have accounted for 10% of net operating expenses.

Item sales comprised 20% of the Company's total sales value for the last three years.

(ii) *Research and Development*
The growth in kit sales has been restricted in recent years by health concerns related to their high lead content. For several years, Norman Epstow has been researching the possibility of developing an alternative substance, which would continue to have the essential hardening characteristics. A major breakthrough was achieved early in 2x05, and it is now probable that the lead content can be reduced to insignificant levels. This is likely to materially increase the level of kit sales.

The Company has incurred the following expenditure in the last two years relating to this project:

- €50,000 in 2x04 – written off to the statement of comprehensive income when incurred, but credited to the same statement in 2x05 and included under trade and other receivables at 31 December 2x05.
- €70,000 in 2x05 – included as a prepayment under trade and other receivables at 31 December 2x05.

In addition, a machine was purchased in February 2x05 for €30,000 to assist in the research project. The Company normally depreciates machinery over five years on a straight line basis, a full year's depreciation being charged in the year of purchase. In view of the successful research developments however, no depreciation has been charged in respect of this machine.

(iii) Sale of Production Rights

In 2x04, Norman Epstow Limited spent €250,000 on the limited rights to produce miniature figures of characters in the film *When We Were Kings,* based on the life of boxer, Muhammad Ali. The production rights were included in the Statement of Financial Position as an intangible asset at 31 December 2x04.

In 2x05 these rights were unexpectedly sold for €550,000, 'a nice killing' according to Norman Epstow. The sales proceeds were included as revenue in the Statement of Comprehensive Income in 2x05, and the intangible asset was retained in Norman Epstow's financial statements.

(iv) Sale of Premises

On 30 November 2x05 Norman Epstow Limited sold a premises for €300,000. This asset had been purchased in 2x02 for €120,000, and was now regarded as surplus to requirements, due to the termination of toy soldier item sales. The premises had been revalued to €200,000 in the financial statements at 31 December 2x03. Depreciation had been provided over a 50-year useful economic life on a straight-line basis with zero residual value. It is the company's policy to charge a full year's depreciation in the year of purchase, and not to depreciate an asset in the year of disposal. The company's other non-current assets are stated at depreciated historical cost.

The premises has been sold subject to an agreement by Norman Epstow Limited that the purchaser would be compensated for the costs of eliminating dry rot, a problem which was identified in an engineer's report commissioned by the purchaser. At 31 December 2x05, the purchaser maintained that the repair costs would amount to €30,000, but on 2 February 2x06 a settlement of €20,000 was agreed.

Norman Epstow Limited has made no provision for repair costs, and has made no record of the disposal of the premises in the 2x05 financial statements.

(v) Joint Venture with Checkmate Limited

On the 1 January 2x05, Norman Epstow Limited entered into a joint venture arrangement with Checkmate Limited. This initiative involved the manufacture of themed chess pieces, to supply the increasing demand for this specialist market. Under the terms of the joint venture agreement, Checkmate Limited will design a range of chess sets, and bear all of the associated design costs. The sets will be manufactured by Norman Epstow, who will take responsibility for all manufacturing and selling costs. It was agreed that sales revenue would be split between Norman Epstow and Checkmate on a 60:40 basis respectively.

During 2x05, Norman Epstow purchased new machinery costing €200,000 for use in connection with the manufacture of chess pieces. Machinery is depreciated over five years on a straight-line basis, with a full year's depreciation being charged in the year of purchase.

Manufacturing costs during 2x05 amounted to €250,000 (including depreciation of machinery), and cash sales of €600,000 were realised during the period. Inventories of chess sets on hand at 31 December 2x05 had been produced at a cost of €100,000 (included in the costs of €250,000 above). These chess sets are 50% complete, and it is estimated that selling costs will amount to €3,000.

(vi)   *Jointly controlled property*

On 1 July 2x05, Norman Epstow jointly purchased an investment property with Telstar Limited. The property, which cost €700,000, is equally owned by both companies. Net rental income for the six months ended 31 December 2x05 amounted to €20,000, all of which was received. The fair value of the property at 31 December 2x05 was €900,000.

Norman Epstow Limited recorded its share of the cost of €350,000 under property, plant and equipment. No further entries have been made.

Requirements:

(a) Explain what adjustments are required to the Draft Financial Statements in respect of the issues outlined in (i)–(vi) above.

(35 marks)

(b) Summarise the journal entries that are necessary in order to implement the adjustments in (a).

(15 marks)

Ignore taxation

_____

Total   **50 marks**

Appendix I

Draft Statement of Comprehensive Income of Norman Epstow Ltd for the Year Ended 31 December 2x05

	2x05 €'000	2x04 €'000
Revenue	1,800	1,300
Cost of sales	(950)	(780)
Gross Profit	850	520
Distribution costs	(120)	(90)
Administrative expenses	(80)	(85)
Other expenses	(100)	(35)
Finance costs	(20)	(18)
Profit before tax	530	292
Income tax expense	(148)	(106)
Profit for the year from continuing operations	382	186

Draft Statement of Financial Position of Norman Epstow Ltd as at 31 December 2x05

	2x05 €'000	2x04 €'000
Assets		
Non-current assets		
Property, plant & equipment	1,693	555
Intangible assets	250	250
	1,943	805
Current assets		
Inventories	269	240
Trade and other receivables	395	322
Cash and cash equivalents	155	130
	819	692
Liabilities		
Current liabilities		
Trade and other payables	365	315
Non-current liabilities		
Term loan	120	135
Net assets	2,277	1,047
Equity		
Share capital	200	100
Share premium	1,150	402
Revaluation surplus	85	85
Retained earnings	842	460
Total equity	2,277	1,047

Norman Epstow owns 60% of the called-up equity share capital, the remaining shares being held by family members and close friends.

RIGHT TYPE GROUP

Introduction

You are an audit senior in a firm of Chartered Accountants, Dartry Maunsell & Co. It is February 2x06 and you are currently reviewing the draft financial statements of the Right Type Group which has recently become a client of your firm.

Right Type Limited is the parent company of a group which operates in the construction industry. The Group has a presence across both the residential and commercial sectors and, based on its progress to date, it is regarded as a serious player in the industry. Right Type Limited was founded by Michael Simpson, who focused in the early years on the residential market. A number of small acquisitions were made subsequently, resulting in the Group diversifying into the commercial sector.

A number of accounting issues have arisen in respect of the audit of the Right Type Group for the year ended 31 December 2x05. The audit manager, Martina O'Sullivan, has requested that you review these issues and send her a memorandum. Your memorandum should set out the appropriate accounting treatment and disclosure in respect of each accounting issue, together with any necessary journal adjustments.

The accounting issues and the draft financial statements are set out in Appendix I and II respectively.

Requirement:

Based on the accounting issues outlined in Appendix I, and the draft financial statements in Appendix II, prepare a memorandum to the audit manager of Dartry Maunsell & Co. in which you undertake the following:

Set out your advice in relation to the accounting treatment, together with any journal adjustments and disclosures required in respect of each of the following accounting issues arising during the 2x05 audit:

(1)	Establishment of Side Type Limited	**11 marks**
(2)	Intangible Assets	**16 marks**
(3)	Commercial contract	**9 marks**
(4)	Expenditure on assets	**14 marks**
		Total 50 marks

including their impact, if any, on:

- (i)   the separate/individual financial statements of the respective companies;
- (ii) the consolidated financial statements of the Right Type Group.

Note: Re-drafted financial statements are NOT required. However, your report should include the journal entries for any accounting adjustments required in respect of each accounting issue.

In their separate financial statements, all companies within the group account at cost for investments in subsidiaries, joint ventures and associates.

Appendix I

Accounting issues arising in respect of the 2x05 Financial Statements

(1) Establishment of Side Type Limited

On 1 April 2x05 Right Type Limited set up Side Type Limited, in conjunction with Bellair Construction. The rationale for the establishment of Side Type Limited was based on the belief that both groups could benefit by joint ownership of a parts warehouse complex located five miles outside Belfast. Both Right Type Limited and Bellair are 50% owners of the ordinary shares in Side Type Limited.

The cost of establishing Side Type Limited amounted to €3 million, which related to the acquisition of a premises. The managing director of Bellair is a personal friend of Michael Simpson but, apart from their joint ownership of Side Type Limited, there is no other relationship between Bellair and the Right Type Group.

From the outset, the management of Side Type Limited was outsourced to Milton Property Care which manages the operation of the warehouse and provides the total staffing requirement. An annual fee of €1 million is paid by both Right Type and Bellair to Milton. Surplus warehouse space is rented to third parties. Total rental income from third parties amounted to €300,000 during the nine months ended 31 December 2x05, and this was shared equally between Right Type Limited and Bellair Construction.

(2) Intangible assets

(a) The Right Type Group has invested heavily in promoting the quality of their brand name over the last three years. €1.2 million was invested in promotion and marketing of the Group brand during 2x03, and the cumulative investment in the Right Type brand has increased annually by 20% since then. On the basis that the brand value significantly enhances that of the Group, it is carried as an asset in the Group Statement of Financial Position. Bellair Construction operates a similar policy in respect of expenditure incurred on brand promotion.

(b) On 1 July 2x05 the Right Type Group paid €3 million for the Well Build brand name, which was previously held by a competitor company. At that time Michael Simpson believed that it had been acquired at a discount of 25% on its market value, and it was included in the Statement of Financial Position of the Right Type Group at its fair value. Consequently, a gain on a bargain purchase was recorded, and this has been maintained in the statement of financial position of the Group. On the basis that the Well Build brand name will increase in value, it is not being amortised in the Group financial statements.

(3) Expenditure on assets

(i) *Replacement of lift*

On 1 January 2x05 Right Type Limited replaced the lift in the company's head office building. The replacement lift cost €300,000, not including future decommissioning costs which were estimated at a present value of €30,000 based on a discount rate of 10%. It was estimated that the lift will have a useful life of 10 years, and a residual value of €20,000 (this is estimated to increase to €35,000, based on prices that are expected to apply in 2016).

The only entry made by Right Type Limited in respect of the new lift is to record it as an addition to land and buildings at its cost of €300,000. Right Type Limited depreciates land and buildings at 2% per annum on a straight line basis.

(ii) *Compliance with fire regulations*

In July 2x05 the Right Type Group invested a total of €400,000 in meeting the requirements of new government fire regulations. This cost has been included in fixtures and fittings, and has been depreciated at 10% on a reducing balance basis. The Right Type Group depreciates land & building at 2% per annum on a straight line basis. Fixtures and Fittings are depreciated by 10% per annum on a reducing balance basis. A full year's depreciation is charged in the year of acquisition in all cases.

The total cost incurred relates to the following items:

	€'000
Repair of fire doors	50
Installation of fire escapes	250
Additional fire extinguishers and miscellaneous safety equipment	100
	400

(4) Revenue Issues

(i) *Sale of residential homes*

During 2x05 the Right Type Group completed the construction of a residential estate of 24 houses. Sales were significantly down on previous developments, primarily as the result of planning permission being granted for a waste management plant adjacent to the estate.

At the 31 December 2x05 sales of 12 houses had been completed at a selling price of €300,000 per house.

Deposits of €20,000 per house had been taken on another four, the sales being dependent on an engineer's report and on the purchaser being able to raise finance. Deposits are refundable if the sale does not proceed.

For the remaining eight, Michael Simpson decided to allow potential purchasers to occupy them on a three-month lease, each lessee paying €1,000 per month in advance. The eight lease agreements were signed on 1 October 2x05, and all lease payments were received at the due date.

On the 2 December 2x05, two of the lessees signed unconditional contracts to purchase a house for €300,000, and it was agreed that the December lease instalment would be set off against the purchase price.

Each house had a completed construction cost of €170,000. No accounting entries have been made in respect of the above.

(ii) *Provision of security service*

While employing security personnel to safeguard the housing estate prior to hand-over, Right Type Limited decided to provide a security service to other developers. On 1 October 2x05 a two-year contract was signed with Property Sites Limited whereby the latter agreed to pay €1,200 monthly in advance, with immediate effect. Should any damage or break-ins occur, Property Sites would be entitled to a full refund of that month's service charge. In addition, they would receive a 50% reduction on the following month's charge.

A break-in occurred on one of Property Sites' properties during November 2x05.

(5) Land

Right Type Limited acquired an area of land several years ago at a cost of €1 million, with a view to using it for house building. The land was revalued to €1.5 million during 2x05. It now appears possible that the planning permission will be rescinded and, in that event, the land would be used for agricultural purposes, at a value of €400,000.

(6) Village Living Concept

During 2x05 Right Type Limited was engaged in finalising plans for the development of a new concept known as 'Village Living', which would involve future housing estates of the group being on a much larger scale, as well as being equipped with services such as a mini-shopping complex. It is expected that the 'Village Living' concept will be finalised in the first quarter of 2x06, and that construction will commence later in 2x06.

During 2x05 Right Type Limited incurred the following costs in connection with the 'Village Living' concept, both of which were charged as expenses:

	€'000
Labour	300
Lease payments on equipment	100

The lease payments relate to the acquisition of a mobile information office. The terms of the lease were as follows:

- Eight half-yearly payments of €100,000, in the primary lease period, commencing in advance on 1 July 2x05. Right Type Limited can retain the information office during the subsequent secondary lease period for an annual payment of €1.

At the date of the inception of the lease, the mobile office had a useful life of five years, and its cash price was €600,000. The present value of the minimum lease payments was also €600,000.

In January 2x06 Right Type Limited announced a 1 for 3 rights issue to finance the further development of the 'Village Living' concept. The rights issue was fully subscribed before the end of February.

Right Type Limited uses the sum of digits method to allocate interest on finance leases.

Appendix II

Draft Statement of Comprehensive Income of the Right Type Group (excluding Side Type Limited) for the year ended 31 December 2x05

	€'000
Revenue	19,100
Cost of sales	(6,900)
Gross profit	12,200
Distribution costs	(700)
Administrative expenses	(250)
Other expenses	(150)
Finance costs	(600)
Profit before tax	10,500
Income tax expense	(750)
Profit for the year from continuing operations	9,750
Other comprehensive income	
Items that will not be reclassified to profit or loss:	
Remeasurements of defined benefit pension plans	(750)
Items that may be reclassified subsequently to profit or loss:	
Cash flow hedges	(250)
Other comprehensive income for the year, net of tax	8,750
TOTAL COMPREHENSIVE INCOME FOR THE YEAR	18,500

All profit and total comprehensive income is attributable to the owners of the parent.

Draft Statement of Financial Position of the Right Type Group (excluding Side Type Limited) at 31 December 2x05

	€'000
Assets:	
Non-current assets	
Property, plant and equipment	6,460
Goodwill	500
Right Type brand	1,728
Well Build Brand	4,000
	12,688
Current assets	
Inventories	1,500
Trade and other receivables	5,000
Amounts recoverable on contracts	6,200
Cash and cash equivalents	1,300
	14,000
Total assets	26,688
Liabilities	
Current Liabilities	
Trade and other payables	5,300
Income tax payable	500
	5,800
Non-current liabilities	
Term loan	200
Deferred income taxes	100
Negative goodwill	1,000
	1,300
Total liabilities	7,100
Net assets	19,588
Equity	
Capital and reserves attributable to	
holders of the Parent	
Share capital	1,000
Share premium	6,000
Revaluation surplus	1,500
Retained earnings	11,088
Total equity	19,588

TRACER GROUP

Introduction

You are an audit senior in a firm of Chartered Accountants, Clarke, Scriven & Co. It is March 2x06 and you are currently reviewing the draft financial statements of the Tracer Group which has recently become a client of your firm.

Tracer Plc is a conglomerate group, comprising a number of subsidiary companies in which dominant influence is exercised by the group parent company, Tracer Limited. The shares of Tracer Plc are listed on the Dublin and London Stock Exchanges.

A number of accounting issues have arisen in respect of the audit of the Tracer Group for the year ended 31 December 2x05. The audit manager, Julie Crimson, has requested that you review these issues and send her a memorandum with your observations and recommendations.

It should be noted that, in their separate/individual financial statements, all companies within the group account at cost for investments in subsidiaries, joint ventures and associates.

It is group policy to measure any non-controlling interest in subsidiaries at the non-controlling interest's proportionate share of the acquired company's identifiable net assets.

The accounting issues are set out below and relevant financial information is set out in Appendix I. It should be assumed that the financial statements are authorised for issue on the 28 February 2x06.

Accounting issues arising in respect of the 2x05 Financial Statements

Issue (a) – Construction of Head Office Building

On 1 January 2x05 Tracer Limited commenced the construction of a new head office building. The new building was scheduled for completion on 30 June 2x05 but, due to a work stoppage from 1 April–30 June, the building was eventually completed on 30 September 2x05.

The various costs paid by Tracer Limited, associated with the construction, are summarised as follows:

Item	1 Jan 2x05 €'000	1 April 2x05 €'000	30 September 2x05 €'000	Total €'000
Site clearance	200			200
Legal fees	70			70
Construction and fitting out		1,600	1,900	3,500
General administration overhead allocation		200	200	400
Total	270	1,800	2,100	4,170

From 1 January 2x05 Tracer Limited paid the amounts outlined, based on architects' certificates obtained at each due date. To finance the construction, Tracer Limited used bank funds obtained for general company use. The interest rate charged on these funds was bank base rate plus 3%. On 1 January 2x05, the bank base rate was 5%, and this increased to 6% on 1 July 2x05.

The total costs of €4.17 million were capitalised as buildings by Tracer Limited at 30 September 2x05. The asset was valued on 31 December 2x05 at €6 million, and was included in the financial statements at that valuation.

Tracer Limited depreciates buildings at 2% per annum on a straight line basis.

Issue (b) – Government Grant

Comps Limited, a 100% subsidiary of Tracer Limited, purchased a machine on 1 January 2x04 at a cost of €500,000. A government grant of €100,000 was received, which was netted off against the machine in the group financial statements at 31 December 2x04. In July 2x05, a government inspector found that Comps Limited had failed to meet the conditions of the grant agreement, relating to employee numbers, and a demand was issued for the repayment of the grant.

Comps Limited has appealed the inspector's decision and, on 28 February 2x06, it was estimated there was a 40% probability that Comps would meet the employment targets, albeit behind schedule, and be able to retain the grant.

It is the policy of the Tracer Group to depreciate plant and machinery at 10% per annum on a reducing balance basis, and depreciation has been charged for 2x05 and 2x04.

Comps Limited has made no entries relating to the repayment of the grant in its financial statements for the year ended 31 December 2x05. Nor has any record been made in respect of the decommissioning costs of the machine, which were estimated, on 1 January 2x04, to amount to €10,000 at the end of the asset's life.

Issue (c) – Share Options

On 31 December 2x03, Tracer Limited issued share options to 10 of its key executives, giving each executive the option to purchase 100,000 shares at €1 per share. The fair value of each option at that date was €0.80.

The exercise of the share options was conditional on the completion of two years' service from 31 December 2x03. The nominal value of the shares of Tracer Limited was 50 cent.

The company's share price on subsequent dates was as follows:

31 December 2x04 €2.70
31 December 2x05 €3.50

In March 2x05, after the 2x04 financial statements were authorised for issue, one of the executives unexpectedly resigned her position in the company. In

April 2x05 a second executive, Patrick Cudmore, was dismissed. Mr Cudmore immediately instigated legal proceedings against Tracer Limited, and it was probable, on the 28 February 2x06, that he would be deemed to have completed the two-year qualifying period of his share option agreement. Legal advice at that time was that he was also likely to be awarded €500,000 in compensation, and that it was possible that this could rise to €900,000.

The eight remaining executives exercised their options on 31 December 2x05.

Issue (d) – Disposal of Shares

On 30 September 2x05, Tracer Limited disposed of 60% of the share capital of Airlight Limited, a subsidiary undertaking in which it had held a 90% stake. The proceeds of disposal amounted to €12 million. Tracer Limited's residual interest of 30% in Airlight Limited allowed it to exercise significant influence over that company.

The 90% stake in Airlight Limited had cost Tracer Limited €9 million on 1 January 2x02, when the identifiable net assets in the statement of financial position of Airlight Limited amounted to €5 million. Goodwill had suffered no impairment loss since acquisition.

Airlight Limited had retained earnings of €3 million on 1 January 2x02, and this figure had increased to €7 million at 31 December 2x04. Airlight Limited had profit after tax of €2 million for the year ended 31 December 2x05.

The fair value of the identifiable net assets of Airlight Limited has always been identical to the carrying value of the identifiable net assets in Airlight Limited's statement of financial position. The fair value of the holding retained was therefore judged to be equivalent to its net asset value.

Requirement:

Issue (a) – Construction of Head Office Building
Review all of the costs involved in the construction of the Head
Office building, and:
– outline your recommended accounting treatment.
– provide relevant journal entries.
– draft Tracer Limited's accounting policy note relating to its treatment of borrowing costs.

17 Marks

Issue (b) – Government Grant

Explain how the Government Grant should be treated in the financial statements of Comps Limited for the year ended 31 December 2x05. Provide relevant journals.

8 Marks

Issue (c) – Share Options

Explain how the share options should be treated in the financial statements of Tracer Limited in 2x04 and 2x05. Provide relevant journals.

9 Marks

Issue (d) – Disposal of Shares

(i) Compute the profit or loss on the disposal of Airlight shares in the *separate financial statements* of Tracer Limited, and provide the relevant journal entry.

4 Marks

(ii) Compute the profit or loss on the disposal of Airlight shares in the *Group Financial Statements*. Provide the relevant journal entry to record this profit, and to reclassify Airlight Limited in the group financial statements.

9 marks

(iii) Disclosure requirements relating to the disposal of Airlight shares in the financial statements of the Group.

3 marks

Total 50 marks

Notes:

- Re-drafted financial statements and consolidated financial statements are **not** required.
- The Tracer Group pays capital gains tax @ 20% on chargeable gains.

Appendix I

Consolidated Statement of Comprehensive Income of the Tracer Group for the year ended 31 December 2x05

	€'m
Revenue	29,000
Cost of sales	(13,800)
Gross profit	15,200
Distribution costs	(3,000)
Administrative expenses	(4,000)
Other expenses	(2,000)
Finance costs	(2,600)
Profit before tax	3,600
Income tax expense	(1,500)
Profit for the year from continuing operations	2,100
Other comprehensive income:	
Items that will not be reclassified to profit or loss:	
Gains on property revaluation	1,000
Items that may subsequently be reclassified to profit or loss:	
Cash flow hedges	450
Other comprehensive income for the year, net of tax	1,450
TOTAL COMPREHENSIVE INCOME FOR THE YEAR	3,550
Profit attributable to:	
Owners of the parent	1,800
Non-controlling interests	300
	2,100
Total comprehensive income attributable to:	
Owners of the parent	3,100
Non-controlling interests	450
	3,550

Consolidated Statement of Financial Position of the Tracer Group as at 31 December 2x05

	€'m	€'m
Assets		
Non-current assets		
Land and buildings	9,600	
Plant and machinery	4,000	
Fixtures and fittings	800	
Investment Property	2,600	
Development costs	1,600	
		18,600
Current assets		
Inventory	3,000	
Trade and other receivables	18,000	
Bank	2,600	
		23,600
Total Assets		42,200
Liabilities		
Current Liabilities		
Trade and other payables	8,400	
Current tax payable	3,200	
		(11,600)
Non-current Liabilities		
Term loan		(7,400)
Deferred income taxes		(200)
		(7,600)
Net assets		23,000
Equity		
Capital attributable to owners of the parent		
Called up share capital		2,000
Share premium		6,000
Revaluation surplus		3,000
Retained earnings		10,800
		21,800
Non-controlling interests		1,200
Total equity		23,000

VERSATILE GROUP

Introduction

You are an audit senior in a firm of Chartered Accountants, Turnbull Bramston & Co. It is February 2x06 and you are currently reviewing the draft financial statements of the Versatile Group which has recently become a client of your firm.

Versatile Plc is a conglomerate group, comprising a number of subsidiary companies in which dominant influence is exercised by the group parent company, Versatile Limited. The shares of Versatile Plc are listed on the Dublin and London Stock Exchanges.

A number of accounting issues have arisen in respect of the audit of the Versatile Group for the year ended 31 December 2x05. The audit manager, Frank DeCourcey, has requested that you review these issues and send him a memorandum with your observations and recommendations.

It should be noted that, in their separate/individual financial statements, all companies within the group account at cost for investments in subsidiaries, joint ventures and associates.

It is group policy to measure any non-controlling interest in subsidiaries at the non-controlling interest's proportionate share of the acquired company's identifiable net assets.

The accounting issues are set out below and relevant financial information is set out in Appendix I.

Accounting issues arising in respect of the 2x05 Financial Statements

Issue (a) – Sale of Subsidiary

On 30 September 2x05 Versatile Limited sold a subsidiary undertaking, Excess Limited, which was no longer considered to be part of the Group's core operations.

Eighty per cent of the shares of Excess Limited had been purchased several years ago for €62 million in cash, when Excess Limited had retained earnings of €25 million. The fair value of Excess Limited's identifiable net assets at that time was €40 million, and these values were fully reflected in the statement of financial position of Excess Limited. To date there has been no evidence that goodwill relating to the acquisition of Excess Limited has become impaired in value.

Excess Limited had retained earnings of €100 million on 30 September 2x05, and the disposal proceeds amounted to €250 million.

Versatile Limited has provided an indemnity to the purchaser against unrecorded taxation or other liabilities. It was estimated at 31 December 2x05 that unrecorded liabilities of approximately €5 million were likely. On 23 February 2x06 (the date on which the financial statements of the Versatile Group were authorised for issue), it was probable that unrecorded liabilities would amount to €10 million.

Goods costing €200 million were sold by Mercer Limited (a wholly-owned subsidiary undertaking of Versatile Limited) to Excess Limited, at a mark-up of 25%, evenly during the year ended 31 December 2x05. Half of the goods purchased by Excess Limited were in that company's inventory at 31 December 2x05.

Issue (b) – Revaluation of Land

Mercer Limited purchased a block of land for €15 million in 2x03 for storage of the Group's building supplies. In 2x04 the area adjacent to the land was identified as the development site for a new shopping centre, and Mercer Limited revalued the land to €80 million at 31 December 2x04, due to its newly acquired development potential. No deferred tax has been provided in respect of the revaluation surplus.

During 2x05 a protest campaign by local residents resulted in the local council withdrawing permission for the commercial development, and at 31 December 2x05 the land was revalued to €30 million. At that point, most of the area was being utilised for storage, with a small section being fenced off for parking by group personnel.

Issue (c) – Contract Work in Progress/Development Site

Minstrel Limited, a wholly-owned subsidiary undertaking of Versatile Limited, has been engaged in the construction sector for several years. On 1 January 2x05 a large site was acquired for the production of retail units, on which construction was scheduled to commence in 2x07. The cost of this site was €20 million and, following an escalation in property values, it was revalued to €35 million at 31 December 2x05.

At 31 December 2x05 a contract for the construction of an office block was in progress. Work on this contract had begun on 1 April 2x05 and was scheduled to be completed on 31 May 2x06. The following information is available in respect of this contract at 31 December 2x05:

Contract 6211Y

	€'m
Costs to date	15.5
Cost of work certified	12.2
Costs to complete	7.7
Value of work certified	15.0
Progress billings	8.8
Amounts received from client	6.3
Contract price	28.5

Issue (d) – Research & Development

During 2x05 Mercer Limited incurred costs of €6.5 million in connection with the development of a new product, 'the wizmo', which will be launched in the marketplace in late 2x06. The results of all tests to date have been positive and market research suggests that 'the wizmo' will be exceptionally well received by consumers.

On 1 January 2x05 a machine was purchased, at a cost of €2.5 million, to carry out final tests on the new product. The Versatile Group depreciates machinery at 20% per annum on a straight line basis, and depreciation on this machine is *not* included in the €6.5 million costs incurred in respect of 'the wizmo'.

Requirements:

Issue (a)
  (i) Explain the correct accounting treatment of the acquisition and disposal of Excess Limited, in the group financial statements **and** in the separate financial statements of Versatile Limited.

 (ii) Set out the journal entries required to reflect your recommended accounting treatment, together with the relevant disclosures.
      The journal entries should cover the period from the date of acquisition to the date of sale and should include:
      – journal entries relating to the group; *and*
      – journal entries relating to the separate financial statements of Versatile Limited.
                                                                      20 marks

Issue (b)
  (i) Explain the correct accounting treatment of the land since its purchase in 2x03.
 (ii) Set out the journal entries required to reflect your recommended accounting treatment.
                                                                       9 marks

Issue (c)
  (i) Explain the correct accounting treatment of the site acquired by Minstrel Limited, and set out relevant journal entries.
 (ii) Explain the correct accounting treatment of the 6211Y contract, and set out the journal entries required.
(iii) Provide Statement of Comprehensive Income and Statement of Financial Position extracts in respect of the 6211Y contract.
                                                                      15 marks

Issue (d)

(i) Explain the correct accounting treatment in respect of the research and development expenditure incurred by Minstrel Limited.

(ii) Set out the journal entries required to reflect your recommended accounting treatment.

6 marks

Total 50 marks

NB Re-drafted financial statements and consolidated financial statements are NOT required. The capital gains tax rate should be assumed at 20%.

Appendix I

Statement of Comprehensive Income of the Versatile Group for the Year Ended 31 December 2x05

	€'m
Revenue	14,500
Cost of sales	(6,900)
Gross profit	7,600
Distribution costs	(1,600)
Administrative expenses	(2,000)
Other expenses	(900)
Finance costs	(1,300)
Profit before tax	1,800
Taxation	(750)
Profit for the year from continuing operations	1,050
Other comprehensive income for the year, net of tax	
Items that will not be reclassified in profit or loss:	
Gains on property revaluation	205
TOTAL COMPREHENSIVE INCOME FOR THE YEAR	1,255

Statement of Financial Position of the Versatile Group as at 31 December 2x05

	€'m	€'m
Assets		
Non-current assets		
Land and buildings	2,300	
Plant and machinery	2,000	
Fixtures and fittings	400	
Investment Property	1,300	
Development costs	800	
		6,800
Current assets		
Inventory	1,500	
Trade and other receivables	9,000	
Bank	1,300	
		11,800
Total assets		18,600
Liabilities		
Current Liabilities		
Trade and other payables	4,200	
Current tax payable	1,600	
		(5,800)
Non-current Liabilities		
Term loan		(1,200)
Deferred income taxes		(100)
		(1,300)
Net assets		11,500
Equity		
Equity attributable to owners of the parent		
Called up share capital		1,000
Share premium		3,600
Revaluation surplus		1,500
Retained earnings		5,400
Total equity		11,500

VORSTER GROUP

Vorster Ltd produces a range of equipment for the automobile industry. In recent years the managing director, Michael Hayes, has led a policy of corporate acquisition and investment in an effort to increase market share. The following are details of acquisitions and disposals:

1. **Acquisition of Motor Factors Limited**

   On 31 October 2x05, Vorster Ltd acquired 80% of the Ordinary Share Capital of Motor Factors Limited for €1,475,000 which was paid in cash. The following information relates to the acquisition:

   - Motor Factors Limited had 200,000 issued ordinary shares of €1 nominal value at 31 October 2x05, along with retained earnings of €850,000.
   - Vorster Limited paid professional fees of €25,000 in evaluating whether it should invest in Motor Factors Limited. In the financial statements of Vorster Limited, this amount was included in the cost of investment.
   - Land and buildings of Motor Factors Limited were worth €100,000 in excess of their book value at 31 October 2x05.
   - There was a disputed tax liability of €180,000 at 31 October 2x05, which was not recorded by Motor Factors Limited. This amount was subsequently confirmed as being due at that date.
   - Vorster Limited intends to carry out a significant reorganisation of Motor Factors Limited. The total cost of this programme is estimated at €90,000, and this has been provided for in Motor Factor Limited's statement of financial position at 31 October 2x05, and

charged in its statement of comprehensive income for the year ended
31 October 2x05.

- It is group policy to value the non-controlling interest at its proportionate share of the subsidiary's fair value of identifiable net assets.

2.   Investment in Auto Parts Limited

On 1 January 2x04, Vorster Limited signed a joint venture agreement with
Magnus Limited to set up a new company, Auto Parts Ltd, which would specialise in buying scrapped cars and storing the parts for sale. Under the terms
of the joint venture agreement, each company received 50% of the ordinary
shares in Auto Parts Limited. Vorster Limited and Magnus Limited each have
three directors on the Board of Auto Parts Ltd, and each of the investing companies participates equally in its management.

At 31 December 2x05 Auto Parts Limited has €300,000 of goods which
were purchased from Vorster Limited. These goods were supplied at a mark-up
of 25% on cost.

3.   Disposal of Cycle Accessories Ltd

As part of its long-term strategy to concentrate on the motorised industry sector, Vorster Limited disposed of a subsidiary company, Cycle Accessories Ltd, on 30 September 2x05. This company had been acquired on
1 January 2x03 at a cost of €200,000 for 100% of its equity shares. At that
time Cycle Accessories Ltd had 100,000 issued ordinary shares of €1 each
nominal value, and retained earnings amounted to €100,000. No goodwill
arose on the acquisition of Cycle Accessories in 2x03.

The proceeds on disposal of Cycle Accessories amounted to €900,000,
all of which was received in cash.

4.   Financial Statements

The financial statements of Auto Parts Limited and of companies in the
Group at 31 December 2x05 are set out below:

Statement of Financial Position

	Vorster Ltd @ 31/12/05 €'000	Vorster Ltd @ 31/12/04 €'000	Motor Factors Ltd @ 31/10/05 €'000	Auto Parts Ltd @ 31/12/05 €'000
Assets				
Non-current assets				
Land & buildings	800	500	300	200
Plant and machinery	800	650	400	180
Investments at cost:				
Shares in Motor Factors	1,500	–	–	–
Shares in Auto Parts	5	5	–	–
Shares in Cycle Accessories	–	200	–	–
	3,105	1,355	700	380
Current assets				
Inventory	1,200	900	350	300
Receivables	1,100	950	400	450
Bank	700	350	250	200
	3,000	2,200	1,000	950
Total assets	6,105	3,555	1,700	1,330
Equity and liabilities				
Ordinary share capital	450	250	200	10
Capital reserves	200	200	–	–
Retained earnings	2,885	1,755	850	770
Total equity	3,535	2,205	1,050	780
Non-current liabilities				
Long-term loan	970	–	–	–
Current liabilities				
Trade and other payables	1,200	1,050	450	400
Current tax payable	400	300	200	150
Total liabilities	2,570	1,350	650	550
Total equity and liabilities	6,105	3,555	1,700	1,330

Draft Statement of Comprehensive Income

	Vorster Ltd y/e 31/12/05 €'000	Motor Factors Ltd y/e 31/10/05 €'000	Autoparts Ltd y/e 31/12/05 €'000
Revenue	4,000	2,100	1,900
Cost of sales	(2,500)	(900)	(800)
Gross profit	1,500	1,200	1,100
Other income	330		
Distribution costs	(350)	(320)	(275)
Administrative expenses	(450)	(280)	(225)
Finance costs	(200)	(20)	(30)
Profit on disposal of Cycle Accessories	700		
Profit before tax	1,530	580	570
Income tax expense	(400)*	(200)	(150)
Profit for the year	1,130	380	420

* Includes €175,000 capital gains tax on the disposal of shares in Cycle Accessories Limited.

5.   **Financial Statements of Cycle Accessories Limited**

The financial statements of Cycle Accessories, which was sold by Vorster Limited on 30 September 2x05, are set out below:

Statement of Financial Position of Cycle Accessories Limited

	31 December 2x04 €'000	31 December 2x05 €'000
Non-current assets		
Land and buildings	200	250
Plant and machinery	150	200
	350	450
Current assets		
Inventory	480	580
Trade and other receivables	300	400
Bank	100	200
	800	1,100
Total assets	1,230	1,630

Equity and Liabilities

Ordinary share capital	100	100
Retained earnings	530	780
Total equity	630	880

Current liabilities

Trade and other payables	450	600
Current tax payable	150	150
Total liabilities	600	750
Total equity and liabilities	1,230	1,630

Statement of Comprehensive Income of Cycle Accessories Ltd for Year Ended 31 December 2x05

	€'000
Revenue	1,000
Cost of sales	(300)
Gross profit	700
Distribution costs	(120)
Administrative costs	(80)
Interest	(100)
Profit before tax	400
Income tax expense	(150)
Profit for the year	250

It should be assumed that the profit of Cycle Accessories Limited accrued evenly over the year.

Requirements:

You are required to prepare the following statements in respect of the **Vorster Group**:

- Statement of Comprehensive Income for the year ended 31 December 2x05.
- Statement of Financial Position as at 31 December 2x05.

Notes:

(i) It should be noted that, in their separate/individual financial statements, all companies within the group account at cost for investments in subsidiaries, joint ventures and associates.

(ii) It is group policy to measure any non-controlling interest in subsidiaries at the non-controlling interest's proportionate share of the acquired company's identifiable net assets.

(iii) All companies in the Vorster Group pay capital gains tax at a rate of 25%.

WEBSTER GROUP

Introduction

You are an audit senior in a firm of Chartered Accountants, Craughwell James & Co. It is February 2x07 and you are currently reviewing the draft financial statements of the Webster Group which is a client of your firm.

Webster PLC is a conglomerate group, comprising a number of subsidiary companies in which control is exercised by the group parent company, Webster Holdings Limited. The shares of Webster Plc are listed on the Dublin and London Stock Exchanges.

A number of accounting issues have arisen in respect of the audit of the Webster Group for the year ended 31 December 2x06. The audit manager, Pamela Deane, has requested that you review these issues and send her a memorandum with your observations and recommendations.

The accounting issues are set out below and the Group's financial information is set out in Appendix I.

Accounting issues arising in respect of the 2x06 Financial Statements

Issue (a) – Deferred Tax

The following details relate to the Group's taxation affairs for the year ended 31 December 2x06:

(i)   During 2x06 the Webster Group generated a large surplus cash balance, which was put on deposit pending a decision on a capital project which was under consideration. Deposit interest accrued in the consolidated Statement of Financial Position at 31 December 2x06 amounted to €2.4 million. The Webster Group will incur a tax charge when the deposit interest is received.

(ii) A land site which the group had purchased in 2x02 for €220 million, was revalued to €370 million at 31 December 2x06. This site is the proposed location for the group's new head office building. This was the first revaluation of this site.

(iii) A building acquired in 2x05 for €25 million was subsequently let to Mercer Limited, a company in which Webster Holdings owns 25% of the equity share capital. At 31 December 2x06, the building was included in the consolidated Statement of Financial Position as an investment property at a valuation of €40 million.

(iv) During 2x06 First Limited sold goods for €36 million to Second Limited. First Limited charged a mark-up of 33% on these sales. Half of the goods are included in the inventory of Second Limited at 31 December 2x06. Both First Limited and Second Limited are 100% subsidiaries of Webster Holdings

(v) Plant and machinery and fixtures and fittings held by the group had a total net book value of €4,820 million at 31 December 2x06. These assets had a total tax written down value of €4,420 million at the same date.

(vi) There were no other temporary differences at 31 December 2x06.

(vii) All companies in the Webster Group pay corporation tax at 12.5%, six months after their accounting year end. The capital gains tax rate is 20%. The balance on deferred tax in the consolidated Statement of Financial Position at 31 December 2x05 amounted to €20 million and this balance has been retained at 31 December 2x06.

Issue (b) – Closure of Division

On the 30 November 2x06 the activities of the export division of First Limited, a 100% subsidiary undertaking of Webster Holdings, were terminated. The division had been loss making for some time, and therefore the decision did not come as a surprise. Fortunately, it was possible to relocate the entire workforce, thus eliminating the necessity for redundancies.

The assets of the division were available for immediate sale, and it was considered to be highly probable that their sale would be completed early in 2x07.

At the 30 November 2x06, the book value of the net assets of the export division (which included buildings carried under the cost model) was €72.6 million. This included inventory of €30 million, which was estimated to have a net realisable value of €26 million at 30 November 2x06.

At the 30 November 2x06, the net assets of the export division had a fair value less costs to sell of €63.9 million.

The export division made a loss before taxation of €96 million for the 11 months ended 30 November 2x06. The loss will be available against other profits of the Webster Group, and will reduce the group taxation charge for 2x06 by €12 million.

Issue (c) – Interest Incurred on Construction of Factory Buildings

On 1 January 2x05, Second Limited, a 100% subsidiary undertaking of Webster Holdings, commenced the construction of a new factory building for its own use. Building work was projected to be completed on 30 June 2x06, but continued until the 30 September 2x06, as work was suspended for three months on 1 April 2x06, due to the discovery of a design error.

Construction costs have been incurred as follows, with payment being made by Second Limited following the submission of an architect's certificate by the contractor:

	Year ended 31 December 2x05	Year ended 31 December 2x06
Site clearance: 1 January certificate	€46 million	–
Purchase of building materials: 1 April certificate	€120 million	€140 million
Direct Labour and production overheads: 1 June certificate	€60 million	€100 million
General overheads: 1 June certificate	€100 million	€80 million

Second Limited paid for the construction costs from its general borrowing facilities. The bank base rate was 5% on 1 January 2x05, and this rate increased to 6% on 1 January 2x06. Second Limited can borrow funds at 2% above the bank base rate.

Second Limited wrote off the interest as an expense in its 2x05 financial statements, but decided to capitalise the interest as part of the cost of the building in 2x06. This change resulted from a revision of IASB rules, requiring the mandatory capitalisation of borrowing costs incurred in connection with the construction of qualifying assets. However, the consolidated financial statements have not been amended for either 2x05 or 2x06 to reflect the new treatment.

Issue (d) – Revenue

First Limited commenced a special promotion during 2x06 whereby customers, whose monthly purchases exceed €100,000, could defer making payment for the goods for one year.

The promotion proved more successful than expected, and total sales for 2x06 on a deferred payment basis amounted to €340 million. First Limited earns a profit margin of 25% on deferred payment sales, and gives a discount of 10% to cash customers.

It is predicted that 4% of customers outstanding at 31 December 2x06 will return their goods to First Limited; 90% of goods returned can be resold, with the other 10% considered to have a zero resale value.

Issue (e) – Financial Instruments

(i) *Loan stock*

Second Limited purchased loan stock in B Limited for €10 million on 1 January 2x06. The loan stock carries no coupon and will be redeemed on 31 December 2x08 for €13,310,000.

The loan stock was purchased with the intention of being held to maturity by Second Limited. The effective interest rate is 10% per annum. No other factor affects the contractual cash flows.

(ii) *Purchase and disposal of shares*

Second Limited purchased shares in Smile plc for €85 million on 1 January 2x06. The shares are held for trading.

At 31 December 2x06, Second Limited has an entitlement to €3 million in respect of dividends declared by Smile plc in November 2x06. The shares held by Second Limited had a fair value of €97 million at 31 December 2x06, and they were sold for €103 million in February 2x07.

Requirements:

Issue (a)

    (i) Compute the correct balance for deferred tax in the consolidated financial statements of the Webster Group at 31 December 2x06.

    (ii) Set out the journal entry required to reflect your adjustment to the deferred tax balance of the Group.

                                                               12 marks

Issue (b)

    (i) Explain the correct accounting treatment of the closure of the export division of First Limited.

    (ii) Set out the journal entries required to reflect your recommended accounting treatment, together with the relevant disclosures.

                                                              10 marks

Issue (c)

    (i) Explain the correct accounting treatment for the interest incurred in respect of the construction of the building by Second Limited. It should be assumed that all interest expenditure relating to the construction is incurred **after the 1 January 2009.**

    (ii) Draft the accounting policy note which will appear in the 2x06 financial statements of Second Limited.

                                                              12 marks

Issue (d)

    (i) Explain the correct accounting treatment in respect of the deferred payment sales by First Limited.

    (ii) Set out the journal entries required in the 2x06 financial statements, to reflect your recommended accounting treatment.

                                                              8 marks

Issue (e)

    (i) Outline the correct accounting treatment in respect of the loan stock purchased by Second Limited, and provide journal entries covering all years from issue to maturity.

                                                              4 marks

(ii) Explain the correct accounting treatment in respect of the shares purchased by Second Limited in Smile Limited. You should also provide journal entries for all transactions between the purchase and disposal dates.

4 marks

Total 50 marks

NB Re-drafted financial statements and consolidated financial statements are *not* required.

Appendix I

Statement of Comprehensive Income of the Webster Group for the Year Ended 31 December 2x06

	€'m
Revenue	3,625
Cost of sales	(1,725)
Gross profit	1,900
Distribution costs	(625)
Administrative expenses	(500)
Finance costs	(325)
Profit before tax	450
Income tax expense	(187)
Profit for the year	263

Other comprehensive income:
Items that will not be reclassified to profit or loss:

Gains on property revaluation	400
TOTAL COMPREHENSIVE INCOME FOR THE YEAR	663

Profit attributable to:

Owners of the parent	263

Total comprehensive income attributable to:

Owners of the parent	663

Statement of Financial Position of the Webster Group as at
31 December 2x06

	€'m	€'m
Assets		
Non-current Assets		
Land and buildings	2,300	
Plant and machinery	4,015	
Fixtures and fittings	410	
Investment Property	335	
Development costs	800	
Financial assets	395	
		8,255
Current Assets		
Inventory	3,550	
Trade and other receivables	3,350	
Bank	700	
		7,600
Total Assets		15,855
Liabilities		
Current Liabilities		
Trade and other payables	4,150	
Current tax payable	1,550	
		(5,700)
Non-current Liabilities		
Term loan		(1,330)
Deferred tax		(20)
		(1,350)
Net Assets		8,805
Equity		
Equity attributable to owners		
of the parent		
Called-up share capital		600
Share premium		4,230
Revaluation surplus		750
Retained earnings		3,225
Total equity		8,805

THE HAYWARD GROUP*

Introduction

You are an audit senior in a firm of Chartered Accountants, Parker Russell & Co.

It is March 2x10 and you are currently undertaking the audit in respect of the 2x09 financial statements of one of your firm's largest clients, the HAYWARD group. The HAYWARD group comprises:

(1) HAYWARD Holdings Ltd ('HAYWARD Holdings'), a holding company employing 25 staff;
(2) HAYWARD Forms Ltd ('HAYWARD Forms'), a manufacturer of business forms and stationery employing 110 staff; and
(3) HAYWARD Flexo Ltd ('HAYWARD Flexo'), a manufacturer of packaging for the food industry, employing 375 staff.

The HAYWARD group is a fourth generation family business. The current Chairman, Jim Hayward, and the Managing Director, Robert Hayward, are father and son. The Board of Directors also includes two further members of the Hayward family, who are no longer directly involved with the day-to-day operation of the business, and one further non-executive director.

The ordinary share capital of HAYWARD Holdings is owned 80% by Jim Hayward, with Robert Hayward owning the balance. HAYWARD Holdings holds 100% of the share capital of HAYWARD Forms and HAYWARD Flexo.

A number of accounting issues have arisen in respect of the audit of the HAYWARD group for the year ended 31 December 2x09. The Senior Partner of Parker Russell & Co., David Parker, has requested that you review the various issues

*2000 Paper 2(i) in the Final Admitting Examination of the Institute of Chartered Accountants in Ireland

and prepare a report for Jim and Robert Hayward which sets out the appropriate accounting treatment and disclosure in respect of each accounting issue, together with any necessary associated journal adjustments. The report is to be issued to Jim and Robert Hayward and discussed at a meeting to take place next week.

The accounting issues and the draft financial statements are set out in **Appendix I** and **II** respectively.

Requirement:

Based on the accounting issues outlined in **Appendix I** and the draft financial statements in **Appendix II**, prepare a report to Jim and Robert Hayward in which you undertake the following:

Set out your advice in relation to the appropriate accounting treatment together with any journal adjustments and disclosures required in respect of each of the following accounting issues arising in respect of the 2x09 audit:

(a)	**Business Rationalisation**	**12 Marks**
(b)	**Head Office Building**	**12 Marks**
(c)	**Flexible Packaging and**	**12 Marks**
(d)	**New Opportunity**	**14 Marks**

including their impact, if any, on:

(i)   the separate/individual financial statements of the respective companies; and

(ii) the consolidated financial statements of the HAYWARD group.

Total 50 Marks

NB   **Re-drafted and consolidated financial statements are not required. However, your report should include journal entries in respect of any accounting adjustments required in respect of each accounting issue.**

It should be noted that, in their separate/individual financial statements, all companies within the group account at cost for investments in subsidiaries, joint ventures and associates.

Appendix I

Accounting Issues Arising in Respect of the 2x09 Financial Statements of the Hayward Group Companies

(a) Business Rationalisation

In early 2x09 HAYWARD Holdings prepared a development strategy for the HAYWARD group which identified the options for the future of the various businesses within the group. The strategy recognised that, as a result of advances in office technology such as laser printers, e-mail and the internet, the business forms and stationery market would rapidly become increasingly competitive and ultimately unprofitable. This had already become apparent in the decreasing profitability of HAYWARD Adhesives, which was a division within Hayward Forms Ltd.

Robert Hayward was tasked with identifying new development opportunities for the group and for preparing an Exit Plan under which the group would withdraw from the adhesives market. The Exit Plan was presented to a meeting of the Board of Directors in October 2x09 and agreed unanimously in principle. Robert Hayward wants the costs of implementing the Exit Plan to be provided for in full in the 2x09 accounts of HAYWARD Forms, although no provision has yet been made. The Exit Plan, which would take approximately 6 months to implement, involves the following:

- **Disposal of continuous printing equipment currently used by HAYWARD Adhesives.** The equipment would have a limited second-hand market locally but is readily saleable via an agent to buyers in the Far East. The agent has already identified an interested buyer. The equipment, which has not been revalued, has a net book value at 31 December 2x09 of €2,000,000 and, on sale, is estimated to realise €1,000,000 before deduction of an agent's fee of 10% of the sale price. The equipment, which has not been used for 6 months due to a lack of orders, is likely to have a limited ongoing value in use to HAYWARD Adhesives whether or not the Exit Plan is implemented. All other equipment in HAYWARD Adhesives can be usefully re-deployed to HAYWARD Forms.

- **Staff redundancies**. A total of 110 staff are currently employed in HAYWARD Adhesives. If the Exit Plan is implemented, 10 staff are likely to be re-deployed elsewhere within the group but the remainder will face compulsory redundancy. The cost of implementing the redundancy programme will be in the region of €1 million. As the Exit Plan remains confidential, the redundancy terms have not yet been discussed with staff or their Union representatives. However, given that the terms are well in excess of statutory entitlements, the Board believes that they are likely to be accepted.

- **Other costs to implement the plan.** In addition to the items noted above, other costs associated with the implementation of the plan, such as legal and professional fees, are estimated at €100,000.

- **Operating losses.** HAYWARD Adhesives is forecast to make a trading loss of approximately €200,000 in the period up to the full implementation of the Exit Plan.

(b) Head Office Building

In order to raise finance for new ventures, HAYWARD Holdings entered into a binding agreement on 31 December 2x09 to sell its head office building to ALPHA INVESTMENTS Ltd for €2 million. This is €500,000 below the estimated open market value of the property, but €500,000 in excess of the net book value at 31 December 2x09.

The terms of the agreement are as follows:

- HAYWARD Holdings will continue to occupy the building for a period of five years.

- At any time during the five-year period HAYWARD Holdings has an option to re-purchase the building whilst ALPHA INVESTMENTS Ltd has an option to sell the property back to HAYWARD Holdings. Under either option, the price will be calculated on the basis of €2 million plus indexation at the bank base lending rate for the period between 1 January 2x10 and the date of re-purchase or re-sale. This option will activate automatically at the end of the five-year period.

- Each quarter in advance, for a period of five years, HAYWARD Holdings will pay rent to ALPHA INVESTMENTS Ltd. The rent will be calculated on the basis of the average daily bank base rate plus 5% charged on €2 million. HAYWARD Holdings will settle directly all other outgoings in respect of the property.

This agreement has not yet been reflected in the draft 2x09 financial statements of HAYWARD Holdings.

ALPHA INVESTMENTS Ltd is a company jointly owned and controlled by Jim Hayward and his wife Iris.

(c) Flexible Packaging

HAYWARD Flexo has been manufacturing packaging for the food industry for a number of years using a range of printing equipment and materials. HAYWARD Flexo has a number of large contracts with supermarket multiples and their suppliers both in Great Britain and in mainland Europe.

1.   *Danish Customer*
     During December 2x09 HAYWARD Flexo manufactured a significant order in respect of DANOBUY, a major customer based in Denmark. The order, which had a sales value of €400,000, was invoiced to DANOBUY on 20 December 2x09 and the sale is reflected in the draft financial statements of HAYWARD Flexo.

     As part of the year-end inventory count procedures on 31 December 2x09, the company's premises and vehicles were inspected by the auditors. During this inspection, a 40 foot container parked at the rear of the company's premises was found to contain the entire DANOBUY order. Although it had been included in pre-year-end despatches on the company's management information system, it was not due for shipment until late January, as DANOBUY did not want to accept delivery until after its year end on 31 January 2x10.

     The materials cost on the DANOBUY order is estimated to be 30% of the sales value. In addition, relevant production overhead is estimated to average in the region of 15% of material cost.

     No adjustments have been made to the draft financial statements in respect of this matter since the inventory count.

2.   *French Customer*
     As part of its recent expansion, HAYWARD Flexo launched a new packaging range that was guaranteed as safe and suitable for direct food contact. The first order for product of €500,000 was invoiced and shipped to a major French customer 'Supermarche' in November 2x09.

However, in early December 2x09, it became apparent that the product was defective and was failing food hygiene tests in France as the ink was leaving traces on food stored within the packaging.

On further investigation by independent experts during December, it was confirmed that the problem had arisen as a result of a combination of defective ink and the manufacturing process which was at temperatures which were insufficient to dry the ink properly. HAYWARD Flexo has been fully involved in the investigation into the causes of the problem which was instigated by its French customer and it is clear that the problems have arisen because of the defective product supplied by HAYWARD Flexo.

Although no subsequent batches produced by HAYWARD Flexo of this food packaging product type have been affected, the initial problem has caused such embarrassment and disruption to Supermarche that it has not paid the initial invoice, has cancelled all further orders with HAYWARD Flexo and refused to accept any more HAYWARD Flexo product.

It is estimated that, to settle the matter in full, will cost HAYWARD Flexo a full refund plus €100,000 in costs incurred by Supermarche. The ink supplier has committed in writing to HAYWARD Flexo that it will meet 50% of the total cost of settlement.

The initial sale of the product to Supermarche has been reflected in the draft financial statements of HAYWARD Flexo but no further entries have been made.

(d) New Opportunity

The group development strategy noted above also recognised the opportunities presented to organisations such as the HAYWARD group by the internet and e-commerce. As a result, on 1 October 2x09, HAYWARD Holdings purchased a 25% equity stake in VIRTUAL INC. ('VIRTUAL'), a local company engaged in Web page design and the re-sale of computer hardware. Robert Hayward believes the fit with VIRTUAL to be particularly appropriate because of HAYWARD group's customer base and in-house design skills, allied to VIR-TUAL's World Wide Web expertise. Both Robert and Jim Hayward have been appointed to the eight-member Board of VIRTUAL and are actively involved in identifying new products and markets for VIRTUAL and in its strategic development.

The purchase of 1 million €1 ordinary shares in VIRTUAL on 1 October 2x09 cost €7.3 million cash. The shares were purchased from Dave Foster, founder and Chief Executive of VIRTUAL, who previously held 100% of the share capital. For Dave Foster the deal provided an opportunity to raise personal funds without losing overall control of the company. Copies of the draft financial statements of VIRTUAL for the year ended 31 December 2x09, which are stated at fair value, are set out in **Appendix III**.

To date, the only entry which has been made in the accounts of HAYWARD Holdings in respect of this transaction is to debit Investments €7.3 million and credit Bank €7.3 million.

Appendix II

Draft Financial Statements for the Year Ended 31 December 2x09

Statement of Financial Position as at 31 December 2x09

	Hayward Holdings Ltd	Hayward Forms Ltd	Hayward Flexo Ltd
	€'000	€'000	€'000
ASSETS			
Non-current assets			
Property, plant and equipment	2,700	2,500	10,000
Investments			
HAYWARD Forms	100		
HAYWARD Flexo	4,000		
VIRTUAL Inc	7,300		
	14,100		
Current assets			
Inventory		200	2,000
Trade Receivables	500	500	3,000
	500	700	5,000
Total assets	14,600	3,200	15,000
EQUITY AND LIABILITIES			
Share capital	500	100	4,000
Retained earnings	900	1,500	6,000
Total equity	1,400	1,600	10,000
Non-current liabilities			
Long-term loans	10,000		
Current liabilities			
Trade creditors	200	800	2,000
Accruals		200	1,000
Bank overdraft	3,000	600	2,000
Total current liabilities	3,200	1,600	5,000
Total equity and liabilities	14,600	3,200	15,000

Statement of Comprehensive Income for the Year Ended
31 December 2x09

	Hayward Holdings Ltd	Hayward Forms Ltd	Hayward Flexo Ltd
	€'000	€'000	€'000
Revenue	1,000	3,500	13,000
Cost of sales	–	800	6,000
Gross profit	1,000	2,700	7,000
Administration costs	750	1,500	2,000
Distribution costs	–	1,000	2,500
Finance costs	750	50	500
Profit/loss before tax	(500)	150	2,000
Income tax expense	–	100	500
Profit/loss for the period	(500)	50	1,500

Appendix III

Draft Financial Statements

Virtual Inc.

Statement of Financial Position at
31 December 2x09

	€'000
Non-current assets	
Property, plant & equipment	7,000
Current assets	
Inventory	–
Trade receivables	2,000
Cash	4,000
Total assets	13,000
Equity and liabilities	
Share capital	4,000
Retained earnings	6,150
Total equity	10,150
Non-current liabilities	
Long-term loans	2,000
Current liabilities	
Trade creditors	150
Bank overdraft	700
Total liabilities	2,850
Total equity and liabilities	13,000

Statement of Comprehensive Income for the Year Ended
31 December 2x09

	€'000
Revenue	80,000
Cost of sales	61,500
Gross profit	18,500
Administration costs	17,000
Distribution costs	–
Interest	900
Profit before tax	600
Income tax expense	
Profit for year	600

BLACK BAY BOATS*

Introduction

It is March 2x13 and you are an audit senior in a firm of Chartered Accountants and Registered Auditors. You are currently undertaking a range of accounting and auditing assignments on behalf of the firm. Each member of staff in the firm is allocated to a practice team for work scheduling and management purposes. One of the audit managers on your practice team is attending a residential training course for a week but has asked you, during his absence, to review some accounting issues which have arisen in respect of the 2x12 audit of one of the firm's clients, BLACK BAY BOATS Ltd ('BLACK BAY BOATS'). In order to provide the background information you need to undertake this work he has sent you an e-mail which contains three attachments:

Appendix I: Background briefing note to BLACK BAY BOATS Ltd.

Appendix II: Draft financial statements for the year ended 31 December 2x12.

Appendix III: Foreign currency rates for the year ended 31 December 2x12.

---

*2001 Paper 2(i) in the Final Admitting Examination of the Institute of Chartered Accountants in Ireland

Requirement

Based on the accounting issues outlined in **Appendix I** and the draft financial statements in **Appendix II**, prepare a memorandum to the audit manager in which you undertake the following:

Set out your advice in relation to the appropriate accounting treatment together with any journal adjustments and disclosures required in respect of each of the following accounting issues arising in respect of the 2x12 audit of BLACK BAY BOATS:

(a)	Investment in Pleasure Craft Inc. ('PLEASURE CRAFT').	**26 Marks**
(b)	Foreign currency loan	**10 Marks**
(c)	Revaluation of showroom	**10 Marks**
(d)	BLACK BAY BOATS: motor craft	**4 Marks**
		Total 50 Marks

including their impact, if any, on:

- the separate financial statements of BLACK BAY BOATS; and

- the consolidated financial statements of the BLACK BAY BOATS group.

Notes:

(1)   Re-drafted or translated financial statements are NOT required. However, your report should include the journal entries in respect of any accounting adjustments required in respect of each accounting issue.

(2)   Ignore taxation implications of recommended accounting adjustments.

(3)   It should be noted that, in their separate/individual financial statements, all companies within the group account at cost for investments in subsidiaries, joint ventures and associates.

It is group policy to measure any non-controlling interest in subsidiaries at the non-controlling interest's proportionate share of the acquired company's identifiable net assets.

Appendix I

Background Briefing Note to Black Bay Boats Ltd

BLACK BAY BOATS is a privately owned company which has been trading for a number of years and is owned and controlled by Mr Jim Kennedy and his wife, Doris, who between them own 100% of the share capital of BLACK BAY BOATS.

BLACK BAY BOATS sells and services luxury motor cruisers from its coastal showroom and stocks a range of craft supplied by some of the world's leading boat manufacturers. The market for luxury motor cruisers, which generally sell for between €100,000 and €1 million each, is closely linked to general economic conditions. As the economy has been growing successfully in recent years BLACK BAY BOATS has expanded and become highly profitable.

Investment in Pleasure Craft Inc ('PLEASURE CRAFT')

The financial success of BLACK BAY BOATS has encouraged Jim Kennedy to look abroad for opportunities to expand the business and, in particular, to seek to break into the lucrative US market. During 2x11 Jim commenced negotiations with a pleasure cruiser distributor based in Miami, Florida, PLEASURE CRAFT. This company is owned and managed by Bill and Ted Powers who are twins in their early 60s and who have been attempting to realise some cash from PLEASURE CRAFT to fund their impending retirement.

The negotiations continued into 2x12 and on 31 March 2x12 BLACK BAY BOATS acquired 10% of the ordinary share capital of PLEASURE CRAFT for 1 million US dollars ($). The initial investment did not give Jim Kennedy any strategic or management input to the company as Bill and Ted Powers were reluctant to dispose of a larger share of the equity until they knew that they could "get on" both professionally and personally with their new fellow shareholder. After six months Bill and Ted Powers agreed to sell a further 40% of the share capital to BLACK BAY BOATS on 30 September 2x12 for $5 million. At the same time Jim Kennedy was appointed Managing Director of PLEASURE CRAFT, assuming day-to-day control over company policy and decision-making, and Bill and Ted Powers effectively withdrew from the management of the business. As a result, BLACK BAY BOATS has taken financial and operational control of PLEASURE

CRAFT. Therefore, at 30 September 2x12 the shareholders of PLEASURE CRAFT were as follows:

Bill Powers	25%
Ted Powers	25%
BLACK BAY BOATS	50%

The net assets of PLEASURE CRAFT in US dollars during 2x12 are as follows:

1 January 2x12	31 March 2x12	30 September 2x12	31 December 2x12
$'000	$'000	$'000	$'000
9,000	9,280	9,840	10,120

(For foreign currency rates refer to **Appendix III**.)

As part of the review exercise undertaken by BLACK BAY BOATS in respect of the second stage investment in September 2x12, the following items were noted:

- A property valuation report dated 1 January 2x12. This had been undertaken by professional valuers acting on behalf of PLEASURE CRAFT which indicated that the company's primary property had increased by $1 million in value compared to its carrying amount in the accounts of PLEASURE CRAFT. The previous valuation was carried out in 2x07.

- A major customer of PLEASURE CRAFT filed for bankruptcy on 1 September 2x12. At that time the customer owed PLEASURE CRAFT $200,000. It is believed that nothing will be recovered from the bad debt.

NB Neither of these items have been adjusted in the net assets or draft financial statements of PLEASURE CRAFT.

- It should be assumed that the fair value of the net assets of Pleasure Craft at 30 September 2x12 is equal to the fair value of the company at that date.

Foreign Currency Loan

The purchase of the investment in PLEASURE CRAFT was funded in part by a 10-year loan taken out by BLACK BAY BOATS, denominated in US dollars and drawn on the First American Bank. The rationale for using a US dollar loan was to try and offset, in part, any adverse movements on the €:$ rate. The loan was drawn down in two parts: $500,000 on 31 March 2x12 and a further $2.5 million on 30 September 2x12. (For foreign currency rates refer to **Appendix III.**)

To date the investment in PLEASURE CRAFT has been accounted for in the books of BLACK BAY BOATS as follows:

Account	Dr. €'000	Cr. €'000
Investment in PLEASURE CRAFT	625	
Bank		312.5
Bank loan		312.5
Investment in PLEASURE CRAFT	3,125	
Bank		1,562.5
Bank loan		1,562.5
Being entries in respect of two investments in PLEASURE CRAFT.		

BLACK BAY BOATS: Showroom Revaluation

BLACK BAY BOATS has been trading from a coastal showroom for the last 13 years. The showroom had been acquired at a cost of €6.25 million. Approximately three years ago there were major concerns over the future suitability of the showroom, as the area where it is located was suffering from significant coastal erosion and prone to potential flooding. However, a major development programme in the area, including the strengthening of coastal defences and the development of a 300-berth marina, has addressed the issues and provided a significant boost to local property values.

Details of recent revaluations undertaken by the same firm of professional valuers in 2x10 and 2x12 on the showroom property are noted below:

- 1 January 2x10 valuation €3 million. This compared to the then carrying value of €5 million. As a result, a €2 million revaluation loss was taken to the statement of comprehensive income of BLACK BAY BOATS.

- 31 December 2x12 valuation €6 million.

The depreciation policy of BLACK BAY BOATS for land and buildings is to write them off straight line over 50 years. A full year's depreciation is charged in the year of purchase. Although the results of the 2x12 revaluation have not yet been reflected in the draft financial statements, the directors have indicated that this valuation should be incorporated in the financial statements.

BLACK BAY BOATS: Motor Craft

BLACK BAY BOATS is a distributor for a number of manufacturers of luxury motor craft. In early 2x12 it obtained distribution rights for a further manufacturer, BAGGIO BOATS ('BAGGIO'), of Italy. The distribution rights are subject to an agreement. At 31 December 2x12 BLACK BAY BOATS had three craft supplied by BAGGIO. The craft were delivered in May 2x12. These craft are all variants of the same basic model with a list price cost at 31 December 2x12 ex BAGGIO of €150,000 each. Under the terms of the agreement this cost, if not previously settled in full, can vary from time to time as BAGGIO reviews prices on a quarterly basis.

At 1 December 2x12 BLACK BAY BOATS had a further BAGGIO craft but this was transferred at the direction of BAGGIO to another dealer in mainland Europe, who had a customer awaiting delivery. The remaining three craft were to be paid for on 1 December 2x12 but BAGGIO has agreed a further six-month no payment period in respect of these craft.

In early 2x12, as part of the agreement, BLACK BAY BOATS paid a refundable inventory deposit to BAGGIO of €100,000. The inventory deposit is the only aspect of this trading relationship which has been reflected in the books of BLACK BAY BOATS. It was accounted for as follows: Cr. Bank and Dr. Trade Payables.

Appendix II

Black Bay Boats Ltd

Draft Financial Statements for the Year Ended
31 December 2x12

Statement of Financial Position as at
31 December 2x12

Assets	€'000
Non-current assets	
Property, plant & equipment	6,500
Investments:	
Pleasure Craft Inc	3,750
Total non-current assets	10,250
Current assets	
Inventory	15,000
Trade receivables	1,000
Cash	5,000
Total current assets	21,000
Total assets	31,250
Equity and Liabilities	
Share capital	1,500
Retained Earnings	19,575
Total equity	21,075
Non-current liabilities	
Long-term loans:	
Bank loans	2,500
US Dollar loan	1,875
Total non-current liabilities	4,375
Current liabilities	
Trade and other payables	5,000
Current tax payable	500
Overdraft	300
Total current liabilities	5,800
Total liabilities	10,175
Total equity and liabilities	31,250

Statement of Comprehensive Income for Year Ended
31 December 2x12

	€'000
Revenue	23,000
Cost of sales	10,000
Gross profit	13,000
Administration costs	2,500
Distribution costs	3,500
Interest	500
Profit before tax	6,500
Income tax expense	1,500
Profit for the year	5,000

Appendix II

Pleasure Craft Inc.

Draft Financial Statements – Stated in US Dollars

Statement of Financial Position as at
31 December 2x12

		US $'000
Assets		
Non-current assets	5,000	
Current assets		
Inventory	8,000	
Trade receivables	1,200	
Cash	500	
Total assets		14,700
Equity and liabilities		
Share capital		2,000
Retained earnings		8,120
Total equity		10,120
Current liabilities		
Trade creditors		4,000
Accruals		280
Overdraft		300
Total liabilities		4,580
Total equity and liabilities		14,700

Statement of Comprehensive Income for Year Ended 31 December 2x12

	US $'000
Revenue	16,000
Cost of sales	8,000
Gross profit	8,000
Administration costs	4,000
Distribution costs	1,000
Interest	500
Profit before tax	2,500
Income tax expense	1,380
Profit for the year	1,120

Appendix III

Foreign Currency Rates for the Year Ended 31 December 2x12

Currency rates over the year were as follows:

Date	$ to €
1 January 2x12	1.50
31 March 2x12	1.60
30 September 2x12	1.60
31 December 2x12	2.00
Average for year 2x12	1.75

TARGET GROUP*

Introduction

It is April 2x02 and you are an audit senior in a firm of Chartered Accountants and Registered Auditors, Brown, Black & Co.

You are undertaking the audit of a major client of the firm, the TARGET group of companies, which comprises:

- TARGET HOLDINGS Ltd ('TARGET HOLDINGS'); and
- TARGET ENGINEERING Ltd ('TARGET ENGINEERING').

TARGET HOLDINGS owns 100% of the share capital of TARGET ENGINEERING. The share capital of TARGET HOLDINGS is owned equally by Derek and Steve Rogers, two brothers who formed the company 10 years ago following successful careers in the engineering sector. The TARGET group designs, manufactures and installs production facilities for pharmaceutical and food processing companies. The group has benefited significantly from the increasing number of such companies developing manufacturing facilities in Ireland.

TARGET HOLDINGS provides administrative and management support to the other group company. TARGET ENGINEERING undertakes the construction and installation of production facilities.

The audit of the TARGET group is 80% complete and a number of accounting issues now require resolution. Your audit manager is due to undertake an assignment review with you in the near future and he has requested that you

*2002 Paper 2(i) in the Final Admitting Examination of the Institute of Chartered Accountants in Ireland

consider the accounting issues which have been identified and make recommendations as to the options for their accounting treatment. The outcome of the
assignment review can then form the basis for a future meeting with the client at
which these matters can be resolved.

The accounting issues requiring resolution are noted below. Draft statements of
comprehensive income and financial position for the two group companies are
set out in **Appendix I.**

Accounting Issues

Issue 1: Head Office Building

Until this year the TARGET group had no permanent Head Office building to
accommodate the design and administrative functions of the group companies.
Instead, connecting temporary buildings had been used to provide office space.
This had been economically prudent as the companies grew and investment was
focused on specialised plant and equipment to generate revenues and improve
productivity. However, the temporary buildings had become increasingly imprac-
tical from an operational perspective and did not create the appropriate impres-
sion for existing and potential customers.

On 1 January 2x01 TARGET HOLDINGS acquired a site adjacent to its main
production facility for the development of a Head Office building. On 1 January
2x01 final plans were agreed and clearance of the site commenced. Construction
continued for approximately a further nine months until the building was available for occupation and came into use on 1 October 2x01.

The various costs incurred by TARGET HOLDINGS associated with the construction during 2x01 are summarised in the table below:

Element	1 Jan. 2x01 € '000	31 Jan. 2x01 € '000	31 Mar. 2x01 € '000	30 Sept. 2x01 € '000	Total € '000
Acquisition of site	2,700				2,700
Legal fees	90				90
Architects' fees	100	60		60	220
Site clearance & preparation		240			240
Construction & fitting out			480	1,200	1,680
General administration overhead allocation			100	100	200
Total	**2,890**	**300**	**580**	**1,360**	**5,130**

From 31 January 2x01 onwards the costs, as indicated in the above table (excluding the general administration overhead allocation), were certified by architects' certificates issued on each date. These were paid by TARGET HOLDINGS on the date of issue using funds drawn down from the company's overdraft facility.

In order to fund the purchase of the site and development of the Head Office building, TARGET HOLDINGS arranged an extension to its bank overdraft facility from €4 million to €8 million for a period up to 31 December 2x01. An arrangement fee in respect of this extension of €28,700 was charged by the company's bankers and debited from the account on 1 January 2x01. The interest rate charged on the facility throughout the year was bank lending base rate plus 4%. On 1 January 2x01 base rates were 5% increasing to 5.75% on 31 March 2x01, at which level they remained until December 2x01. The use of the extended bank overdraft was intended as a temporary funding mechanism to cover the period of construction only.

In the non-current assets of TARGET HOLDINGS at 31 December 2x01 the building has been capitalised at a total cost of €4,820k comprised as follows:

- Acquisition of site €2,700k
- Site clearance and preparation €240k
- Construction and fitting out €1,680k
- General administration overhead allocation capitalised €200k.

All the other costs noted in the table on the previous page have been expensed to the statement of comprehensive income. No depreciation has been charged to date on the Head Office building in this financial year (2x01) although the depreciation policy of the company in respect of land and buildings is to write them off, straight line, over 50 years from the date of coming into use.

Interest Capitalisation

Derek Rogers is an engineer but throughout the trading history of the group he has taken Board level responsibility for company accounts and financial issues, in conjunction with the in-house book-keeper/accountant. During the course of the audit Derek has indicated to you that he is aware of other companies which have capitalised interest charges on construction projects and he would like the advice of the company auditors in this respect with regard to the Head Office building.

Construction & Fitting Out

The construction and fitting out of the Head Office building was undertaken by ACORN DEVELOPMENTS Ltd ('ACORN'). ACORN is a company which is 40% owned by Steve Rogers and it undertakes general construction assignments for a number of clients. As a result of the commitment required by his involvement in the TARGET group, Steve Rogers has no executive role within ACORN nor is he a Director of the company.

Tenders for the construction and fitting out work were sought from four potential contractors. Three contractors, including ACORN, submitted tenders. All of the submitted tenders met the required technical and build quality criteria. The ACORN tender, which was ultimately successful at €1.680 million, was the highest priced received and was €400,000 higher than the lowest tender submitted.

Issue 2: Head Office Building Disposal

On 31 December 2x01 the recently completed Head Office building was disposed of to FITZPATRICK PROPERTIES Ltd ('FITZPATRICK') for €6.5 million. The terms of the disposal were as follows:

- FITZPATRICK pays €6.5 million to TARGET HOLDINGS on 31 December 2x01;
- TARGET HOLDINGS enters into a five-year agreement with FITZPATRICK to occupy the property at an annual rent payable quarterly in advance. The rent is €575,000 per annum;
- TARGET HOLDINGS has no option to repurchase the property; and
- TARGET HOLDINGS is responsible for all repairs and upkeep during the lease period.

In December 2x01 TARGET HOLDINGS commissioned a valuation of the property by its property advisers. The property advisers estimated the open market value (fair value) of the property to be €5.5 million.

NB The only entry to have been made in the draft accounts of TARGET HOLDINGS in respect of this transaction is to Dr. Bank Overdraft €6.5 million; Cr. Other Payables €6.5 million.

Issue 3: Third-Party Claim

TARGET ENGINEERING has two trading divisions, the Pharmaceutical Division and the Food Processing Division. The divisions specialise respectively in the construction and commissioning of production facilities either for pharmaceutical or for food processing companies. The Pharmaceutical Division has experienced some problems in relation to an installation carried out during 2x01. As a result, the client involved is pursuing a claim against TARGET ENGINEERING for costs and consequential loss. The key details relating to the claim are as follows:

Client A
TARGET ENGINEERING was the sole building contractor on this project. The work, which involved the construction of a new manufacturing suite, was undertaken in the first quarter of 2x01 and the total value of the contract was €500,000.

Since the work was undertaken, Client A, a pharmaceutical company, has been unable to obtain suitable regulatory approval for the manufacturing suite as the test batches produced in the suite are showing signs of contamination. This contamination is attributed to the air conditioning system, installed by TARGET ENGINEERING, importing dust particles into the suite. On 30 June 2x01 Client A instituted legal proceedings against TARGET ENGINEERING for recovery of the full contract value plus a consequential loss claim of €250,000.

The legal case is still pending and the limit of TARGET ENGINEERING's insurances in this respect totals €400,000. Solicitors and expert witnesses appointed by TARGET ENGINEERING have privately advised that it is probable that Client A's action will be successful. TARGET ENGINEERING's insurers have reviewed the circumstances in detail and have indicated in writing to TARGET ENGINEERING that they will offer €400,000 in part-settlement of the claim and in full settlement of their liability as insurers under the policy.

Issue 4: Divisional Reorganisation

The TARGET group continually evaluates the business performance of the group companies to ensure focus, effort and resources are concentrated on those areas that can generate maximum return for the group. Experience and results over the last 18 months have clearly indicated that the Pharmaceutical Division of TARGET ENGINEERING is proving to be less profitable than the Food Processing Division but is utilising the same resources and capital.

As a result, during November 2x01, a Divisional Reorganisation Plan was formulated to focus the future trading activities of TARGET ENGINEERING exclusively on customers in the food processing sector. This Divisional Reorganisation Plan will have an impact on the staff, non-current assets and other resources which, to date, have been dedicated to the Pharmaceutical Division.

The details of the plan have already been discussed with, and communicated to, the relevant employees and their union representatives. It is widely known by the company's competitors, customers and suppliers that TARGET ENGINEERING is no longer tendering for future contracts in the pharmaceutical sector. The timetable within the Divisional Reorganisation Plan assumes implementation commencing in February 2x02 with completion by June 2x02.

The key features of the Divisional Reorganisation Plan are as follows:

- 30 staff facing compulsory redundancy at a cost to the company of €500,000;
- 20 staff re-tasked to the Food Processing Division – training costs to convert €50,000;
- Investment in new systems to support expanded Food Processing Division €100,000.

None of the costs have been incurred yet but Derek Rogers anticipates that he will create a restructuring provision in the financial statements of the coming year i.e. 31 December 2x02 for €650,000 to cover, in full, the costs of implementing the plan.

In addition, TARGET ENGINEERING has specialist tooling and plant and equipment which was previously utilised by the Pharmaceutical Division with a net book value in the draft financial statements of €1 million. Some of this equipment can be redeployed to the Food Processing Division but the remainder, which has a net book value of €250,000, can only be sold on the second-hand market for an estimated €50,000. An outline agreement to sell the equipment at the estimated sale value has already been made with a prospective buyer.

Requirement:

Based on the accounting issues outlined above and the draft financial statements in **Appendix I**, prepare a memorandum to the audit manager in which you undertake the following:

Issue 1

(i) Review all the direct and associated costs involved in the construction of the Head Office building and identify which should be capitalised in the financial statements of TARGET HOLDINGS.

5 Marks

(ii) Set out the circumstances in which interest on borrowings may be capitalised and calculate the appropriate amount of interest that should be capitalised in the financial statements of TARGET HOLDINGS in the year ended 31 December 2x01, together with any appropriate disclosures.

9 Marks

(iii) What, if any, is the impact on the financial statements of TARGET HOLDINGS of the contract for the construction and fitting out being awarded to ACORN.

6 Marks

Issue 2

Set out how the disposal of the Head Office building should be reflected in the financial statements of TARGET HOLDINGS for the year ended 31 December 2x01 together with any appropriate disclosures.

12 Marks

Issue 3

Set out the impact, if any, of the third-party claim on the financial statements of TARGET ENGINEERING for the year ended 31 December 2x01.

6 Marks

Issue 4

Set out the impact, if any, of the Divisional Reorganisation Plan on the financial statements of TARGET ENGINEERING for the year ended 31 December 2x01.

12 Marks

Total 50 Marks

NB Re-drafted financial statements are not required. However, your report should include the journal entries in respect of any accounting adjustments required in respect of each accounting issue.

Ignore any taxation implications of recommended accounting adjustments.

Appendix I

Draft Financial Statements for the Year Ended
31 December 2x01

Statement of Financial Position as at
31 December 2x01

	Target Holdings 31 December 2x01 €'000	Target Engineering 31 December 2x01 €'000
Non-current assets		
Tangible assets	8,500	27,000
Investments (TARGET ENGINEERING)	1,000	
	9,500	27,000
Current assets		
Inventory		3,000
Trade receivables	2,000	5,000
Inter-company	200	
Cash	100	200
	2,300	8,200
Total assets	11,800	35,200
Equity and liabilities		
Current liabilities		
Trade payables	200	7,000
Accruals/other payables	6,700	1,000
Inter-company	–	200
Overdraft	3,000	1,000
	9,900	9,200
Non-current liabilities		
Bank loans	500	3,000
Total liabilities	10,400	12,200
Equity		
Share capital	1,200	1,000
Retained Earnings	200	22,000
Total equity and liabilities	11,800	35,200

Statement of Comprehensive Income for Year Ended
31 December 2x01

	Target Holdings €'000	Target Engineering €'000
Revenue	1,750	25,000
Cost of sales	100	12,500
Gross profit	1,650	12,500
Administration costs	1,200	4,000
Distribution costs		3,000
Finance costs	500	500
Profit/(loss) before tax	(50)	5,000
Tax		1,000
Profit/(loss) for the year	(50)	4,000

THE MAGNA GROUP*

Introduction

You are an audit senior in a firm of Chartered Accountants, Campbell Wilson & Co. It is March 2x07 and you are currently undertaking the audit in respect of the 2x06 financial statements of one of Campbell Wilson's largest clients, the MAGNA group. The MAGNA group of companies develops, manufactures and sells specialist scanning and imaging equipment for use in medical and security related work.

MAGNA HOLDINGS Ltd ('MAGNA HOLDINGS') was formed over 30 years ago by two founders, Dr Patrick Bellamy and Dr Harry Shearer, who originally met whilst senior lecturers at the physics department of a renowned local university. The company was formed as part of a university-backed drive to realise the commercial applications of world leading and unique research undertaken on campus. Since then the holding company has formed several new and very successful trading companies which have enjoyed worldwide commercial success. The share capital of MAGNA HOLDINGS is held by the two founding partners together with a further colleague brought into the company to deliver sales and marketing expertise. Finally, a small amount of the share capital is held indirectly by the university.

*2003 Paper 2(i) in the Final Admitting Examination of the Institute of Chartered Accountants in Ireland

The MAGNA group is structured as follows:

MAGNA HOLDINGS – holding company as 'umbrella' for other group activity.

- 100% subsidiary – MAGNA SECURITY Ltd ('MAGNA SECURITY') – develops and manufactures products for security applications.

- 100% subsidiary – MAGNA MEDICAL Ltd ('MAGNA MEDICAL') – develops and manufactures products for human medical applications.

- 80% subsidiary – CLEAR SCAN Inc. ('CLEAR SCAN') – a Ruritanian company which develops and manufactures scanning and imaging products for applications in the gaming and casino industries in Ruritania.

- 70% investment in SUREGUARD Ltd ('SUREGUARD') which operates security contracts in the public and private sectors.

A number of accounting issues have arisen in respect of the audit of the group financial statements for the year ended 31 December 2x06. The senior partner of Campbell Wilson & Co., David Campbell, has requested that you review the various issues and prepare a report for the directors of the MAGNA group which sets out the appropriate accounting treatment and disclosure in respect of each accounting issue together with any necessary associated journal adjustments. The report is to be issued to the directors and discussed at a meeting to take place next week. The accounting issues and the draft financial statements are set out in **Appendix I** and **Appendix II** respectively.

Requirements:

Issue (a)

(i)   Explain how the investment in SUREGUARD should be treated and disclosed in the separate company financial statements of MAGNA HOLDINGS and in the consolidated financial statements of the MAGNA group for the year ended 31 December 2x06.

14 marks

(ii) Set out the journals required to reflect your recommended accounting treatment under (i), together with any journals and disclosures arising from transactions between MAGNA SECURITY and SUREGUARD during the year ended 31 December 2x06.

6 marks

Issue (b)

(i)   Set out how the investment in CLEAR SCAN should be accounted for in the financial statements of MAGNA HOLDINGS at the date of acquisition and calculate the goodwill arising on consolidation.

7 marks

(ii) Set out what impact, if any, the reduction in actual and forecast profits of CLEAR SCAN has on the carrying value of the investment and goodwill at 31 December 2x06.

8 marks

Issue (c)

Set out the impact, if any, of the withdrawal of the Canadian competitor on the carrying value of the 'mothballed' equipment in the financial statements of MAGNA SECURITY for the year ended 31 December 2x06.

7 marks

Issue (d)

Set out how Projects A and B should be accounted for in the financial statements of MAGNA MEDICAL for the year ended 31 December 2x06.

8 marks

Total 50 Marks

NB: Re-drafted financial statements and consolidated financial statements are not required.

- Ignore any taxation implications of recommended accounting adjustments.
- It should be noted that, in their separate/individual financial statements, all companies within the group account at cost for investments in subsidiaries, joint ventures and associates.
- It is group policy to measure any non-controlling interest in subsidiaries at the non-controlling interest's proportionate share of the acquired company's identifiable net assets.

Appendix I

Accounting Issues Arising in Respect of the Audit of the Financial Statements of the MAGNA Group for the Year Ended 31 December 2x06

Issue (a) – SUREGUARD Ltd

As part of the commercial development of the group, MAGNA HOLDINGS has been strategically seeking expansion into new but related business areas. On 1 January 2x06 MAGNA HOLDINGS, together with another company, STANDARD SECURITY, formed a new company, SURE-GUARD Ltd ('SURE-GUARD'), to bid for security contracts at ports, airports and other public and private buildings. Strategically, this is believed to represent a good 'fit', with MAGNA HOLDINGS delivering the equipment, infrastructure and finance for the contracts whilst STANDARD SECURITY sources the security manpower and day-to-day management to deliver the operational requirements of the contracts. During its first full year of trading SUREGUARD has successfully commenced a number of major contracts at retail stores and regional airports and the initial performance of the company has been slightly ahead of expectations.

MAGNA HOLDINGS holds 70% of the share capital of SUREGUARD with 30% held by STANDARD SECURITY. Both MAGNA HOLDINGS and STANDARD SECURITY are fully involved in the strategic development of SUREGUARD and each company has two seats on the executive board. Voting rights of the company are split equally between the two investors and, although not subject to any written agreement, it has been agreed and practised to date that either party can exercise a veto over key decisions. The intention is that in future years if the company trades profitably then the two investor companies will receive dividends from SUREGUARD.

From your audit work you are also aware that MAGNA SECURITY has sold equipment to SUREGUARD, which is being utilised on the various security contracts. This equipment was invoiced to SUREGUARD in February 2x06 at €1.4 million sales value and is being carried forward at this amount less depreciation. The cost to MAGNA SECURITY of these items was €1 million. A debtor remains in the books of MAGNA SECURITY at 31 December 2x06 of €250,000 in respect of this transaction.

Issue (b) – CLEAR SCAN Inc.

MAGNA HOLDINGS purchased 80% of the share capital of CLEAR SCAN on 1 January 2x06. Negotiations to purchase a stake in the company had commenced during the summer of 2x05 and had eventually been finalised in December 2x05 with the deal finally completing on 1 January 2x06. The purchase price of 18 million Ruritanian dollars was determined based on the estimates of future profitability performance of CLEAR SCAN over the next four years prepared by the directors of MAGNA HOLDINGS and their advisers. During December 2x05 the directors of MAGNA HOLDINGS estimated the trading profits before interest and tax of CLEAR SCAN as follows over the next four years:

Financial Year End	Profit Estimate R$'000
31 December 2x06	3,750
31 December 2x07	3,750
31 December 2x08	7,500
31 December 2x09	7,500

Total profits over the four-year period were therefore estimated to be R$22.5 million and this was used to derive the purchase price of the company. At 31 December 2x05 the net assets of CLEAR SCAN after fair value adjustment totalled R$10.5 million. The R$ rate has remained consistent throughout this period at 1.5:€1.

Unfortunately, as a result of adverse trading conditions during the first year's trading under the ownership of the MAGNA group, the trading performance of CLEAR SCAN has not matched the expectations prior to the take over. Profit before interest and tax for the year to 31 December 2x06 was R$500,000 and the estimates for the next three years have been revised downwards as follows:

Financial Year End	Profit Estimate R$'000
31 December 2x07	3,125
31 December 2x08	5,000
31 December 2x09	6,375

It may be assumed that the recoverable amount of CLEAR SCAN varies in proportion to expected future profit. Ignore discounting.

Issue (c) – Portable Metal Detectors

Three years ago the majority of MAGNA SECURITY's turnover and profits were derived from the manufacture and sale of portable metal detectors. However, in November 2x02 a rival Canadian company entered the market with cheaper and more easily portable equipment which utilised pioneering new technology capable of detecting a wider range of metals and materials even if present in smaller quantities. This 'new technology' effectively rendered MAGNA SECURITY's products uncompetitive and virtually unsaleable. As a result of an impairment review prompted by the impact on trading of the Canadian competitor, MAGNA SECURITY wrote down the value of its Portable Metal Detector production line on the grounds of impairment and focused on other areas of its operations.

The equipment concerned comprised a production line and associated tooling purchased and first used in operation on 1 January 2x00 with a cost of €2 million. The equipment was depreciated straight line over 10 years and with a full year's depreciation charged in the year of acquisition.

On 1 January 2x03 MAGNA SECURITY took the decision to provide in full for the then NBV of the equipment, as the equipment was very specialised and had no value on the open market and could not be used in any other of the company's operations. The equipment was 'mothballed'.

In June 2x06 the Canadian company was forced to recall and withdraw its products from sale as a result of health scares experienced by operators of the equipment. Consequently, since June 2x06 MAGNA SECURITY has been inundated with enquiries and orders for its original market leading product and production recommenced on 1 October 2x06 using the previously 'mothballed' production line.

Issue (d) – Development Projects

MAGNA MEDICAL has a research facility dedicated to developing new technology for use in specialised imaging equipment with medical applications. The company has a consistently applied accounting policy for capitalising relevant development expenditure, which is then released over the life of the associated products. During the 2x06 financial year two major new projects have commenced as follows.

Project A
During 2x06 MAGNA MEDICAL commenced development of a new range of portable medical scanners which use mobile phone technology to link users (nurses and doctors) located in remote areas to consultants based in regional specialist centres. The potential applications and commercial returns are believed to be exceptional and are forecast to significantly exceed development costs.

Given the strategic importance of such a product, funds are available to complete the work. According to the detailed project plans and milestones the work will take a further 12 months to complete. Costs incurred to date total €450k with a further €1.2 million of investment required to complete the work during 2x07.

Project B
During 2x06 the company commenced contract development work for another medical product company, STAR MONITORS Ltd ('STAR MONITORS'), developing circuitry for use in human heart monitors. Costs incurred by MAGNA MEDICAL plus an agreed mark-up profit will be paid in full by STAR MONITORS. MAGNA MEDICAL has to date incurred €250k of costs in this project. STAR MONITORS made a payment on account of €100k in respect of this work in December 2x06 although MAGNA MEDICAL has not yet invoiced any of this work to STAR MONITORS.

To date, the costs relating to both these products have been booked to deferred development expenditure in the statement of financial position of MAGNA MEDICAL. The payment from STAR MONITORS has been accounted for by:
      Dr. Bank €100k
      Cr. Capitalised Development Costs €100k

Appendix II

Draft Financial Statements

	Magna Holdings Ltd	Magna Security Ltd	Magna Medical Ltd
	31 December 2x06	**31 December 2x06**	**31 December 2x06**
	€'000	€'000	€'000
Assets			
Non-current assets			
Property, plant and equipment	1,000	15,000	11,000
Intangible assets			2,000
Investments			
In MAGNA SECURITY Ltd	1,000		
In MAGNA MEDICAL Ltd	1,000		
In CLEAR SCAN Inc.	12,000		
In SUREGUARD Ltd	140		
	15,140	15,000	13,000
Current assets			
Inventories		2,500	3,250
Trade receivables	200	5,000	4,000
Inter-company	300		300
Debt due from SUREGUARD	–	250	–
Cash	500		100
	1,000	7,750	7,650
Total assets	16,140	22,750	20,650
Equity and liabilities			
Share capital	1,000	1,000	1,000
Retained earnings	10,640	8,950	13,400
	11,640	9,950	14,400
Non-current liabilities			
Bank loans	3,000	1,000	1,250
Current liabilities			
Trade payables	1,000	4,000	3,000
Accruals	200	1,000	750
Inter-company	300	300	–
Overdraft	1,000	6,500	1,250
Total equity and liabilities	16,140	22,750	20,650

	Year Ended 31 December 2x06	Year Ended 31 December 2x06	Year Ended 31 December 2x06
	€'000	€'000	€'000
Revenue	2,750	22,000	13,000
Cost of sales	300	12,000	8,000
Gross profit	2,450	10,000	5,000
Administration costs	300	4,000	1,000
Distribution costs	100	2,000	1,000
Finance costs	500	1,000	500
Profit before tax	1,550	3,000	2,500
Income tax expense	250	1,000	1,000
Profit for the year	1,300	2,000	1,500

Draft Financial Statements of Clear Scan Inc. – Stated in Ruritanian Dollars

Statement of Financial Position

Clear Scan Inc.

31 December 2x06

	R$'000
Non-current assets	8,500
Current assets	
Inventory	4,300
Trade receivables	
Cash	
Total assets	12,800
Equity and liabilities	
Share capital	2,000
Retained earnings	8,800
	10,800
Current liabilities	
Trade payables	1,500
Accruals	
Overdraft	500
Total equity and liabilities	12,800

Statement of Comprehensive Income

**Year Ended
31 December 2x06**

	R$'000
Revenue	20,000
Cost of sales	17,750
Gross profit	2,250
Administration costs	1,000
Distribution costs	750
Finance costs	50
Profit before tax	450
Income tax expense	150
Profit for the year	300

Draft Financial Statements of Sureguard Ltd.
Statement of Financial Position

Sureguard Ltd

31 December 2x06

	€'000
Non-current assets	9,100
Current assets	
Inventory	50
Trade receivables	1,700
Cash	150
Total assets	11,000
Equity and liabilities	
Share capital	200
Retained earnings	200
	400
Long-term liabilities	
Bank loans	10,000
Current liabilities	
Trade payables	100
Debt due to MAGNA SECURITY	250
Accruals	50
Overdraft	200
Total equity and liabilities	11,000

Statement of Comprehensive Income

**Year Ended
31 December 2x06**

	€'000
Revenue	9,000
Cost of sales	7,000
Gross profit	2,000
Administration costs	400
Distribution costs	120
Interest	1,180
Profit before tax	300
Income tax expense	100
Profit for the year	200

HARRINGTON MOTORS LIMITED*

Introduction

HARRINGTON MOTORS Ltd ('HARRINGTON') is a successful Irish car dealership, which has grown rapidly over the last few years. The company acts primarily as an outlet for specific models of cars, but also has a repairs workshop. The company was founded by Mr Nick Harrington and has traded profitably for the last 30 years. Nick has recently retired and his son, Patrick, has taken over the business. Patrick is keen to expand the business and pursue new opportunities. He has asked you, as his newly appointed Financial Controller, to advise him on various accounting matters in the form of a memorandum. The financial year end of the company is 31 December.

The accounting issues are set out below and relevant financial information is set out in **Appendix I.**

*2004 Paper 2(i) in the Final Admitting Examination of the Institute of Chartered Accountants in Ireland

Issue (a) – New Dealership

HARRINGTON has been offered the opportunity to act as a dealer for a new make of environmentally friendly car, the Green Machine ('GM'). As the GM is relatively new to the Irish market place, Patrick Harrington has managed to negotiate favourable terms for the franchise in order to mitigate the risk to the company. Under the terms of the agreement, HARRINGTON will take delivery of the cars, without paying a deposit, and can return any or all of the cars to the manufacturer without penalty at any stage. This ensures that, if the vehicles are not popular with consumers, HARRINGTON has a way of transferring the cars back to the manufacturer. Patrick Harrington feels that he has little to lose from a commercial viewpoint and is keen to pursue this arrangement.

The book-keeper has included the cars purchased, at a total cost of €200,000, as purchases of inventory in the accounts. Two cars have been sold, at a total value of €40,000, and these have been included as revenue in the year. Each of the cars that has been sold had an original cost of €15,000 and the remainder of the cars are included in the year-end inventory figure.

Issue (b) – Premises

In the past, HARRINGTON operated from leased premises, and continued to do so from January to November 2x05, paying a monthly rental of €30,000. During December 2x05, the business re-located its entire operations to new purpose-built premises. The lease on the old premises runs until 31 December 2x07 and the lease does not permit re-letting the premises to another user. The former premises are now vacant and unused. Lease payments up to 31 December 2x05 have been charged as an expense in the statement of comprehensive income.

Patrick had spent several years trying to find alternative premises for the company without success. In the end, he paid a business colleague, Mr Matthew Reid, who is a qualified valuer, the sum of €30,000 to assist him in selecting an appropriate site for building a purpose-built showroom and workshop. The site was eventually purchased in January 2x05 and the building was completed on 1 November 2x05.

The following costs have been capitalised in the accounts for year ended 31 December 2x05:

	€
Site selection (as described above)	30,000
Architects' fees	20,000
Lost revenue during two-week closure to facilitate move................................	100,000
Purchase of land	980,000
Legal fees re: purchase of land	50,000
Building costs	500,000
Total costs	1,680,000

The book-keeper has charged two months' depreciation on the total costs capitalised in the accounts. The depreciation policy for buildings in HARRINGTON is to charge a full year's depreciation in the year of acquisition at 2% straight line and none in the year of disposal.

On 31 December 2x05, Mr Reid advised Patrick that the showroom and workshop were worth €1,700,000 for their current purpose. However, due to new planning developments within the last year, the site is now worth well in excess of this amount if developed for residential property. The current value on the open market for residential purposes would be around €1,900,000.

Patrick is keen to strengthen the statement of financial position of HARRINGTON and would like your advice on how to incorporate these valuations in the financial statements.

Issue (c) – New Equipment

Patrick acquired new equipment for spraying cars at a cost of €200,000 in September 2x05. The equipment was tested by staff in September 2x05 to ensure that it would function correctly after implementation. As a result of the testing, various adjustments were made to the equipment, without which the equipment would not function correctly. The cost associated with this period was approximately €25,000. During the last three months of 2x05 the equipment was available for use but, due to a lack of marketing, it was only used intermittently. The monthly cost of running the equipment during that three-month period was €15,000.

Patrick is keen to capitalise the costs associated with this equipment, although his bookkeeper has expensed the costs to date as follows:

Dr	Plant & equipment expenses	€70,000
Cr	Bank	€70,000

He would like your advice on the possibility of capitalising these costs and the journal entries required.

Issue (d) – New Customer

Patrick has been approached by a local firm, Smith Motors Ltd, which currently has an arrangement with one of Patrick's competitors, in relation to its fleet of 30 company cars. The cars are currently traded in every three years, with a one-off payment being made at the date of trade-in for each car. The owner of the local firm has decided to consider alternative methods of financing his fleet, and would like to consider easing his cash flow burden by means of contract hire.

In order to provide this service, Patrick would need to purchase 30 new cars from the relevant manufacturers and to trade these in every three years. However, he feels that he should get a good deal on trade-ins due to his long-standing relationships with the relevant manufacturers.

The hire period would commence on 1 April 2x06 and run for three years. The schedule of inflows would be as follows:

1 April 2x06	**€200,000**
1 April 2x07	**€100,000**
1 April 2x08	**€75,000**

Patrick would like your advice regarding the accounting treatment and disclosure of these transactions.

Issue (e) – Potential Acquisition

Patrick Harrington has been approached by a businessman, John Coulter of FOCUS Ltd ('FOCUS'), who has asked him to consider investing in his business. FOCUS is a parts wholesaler and Patrick Harrington feels that this would be a useful investment and would add another dimension to his own business. The accounts of FOCUS are shown in **Appendix I.**

Included in the accounts of FOCUS is a property with a net book value of €1,675,500 which has a market value of €2,000,000.

Patrick has reviewed the accounts of FOCUS, and has discussed various alternative methods of investment with John Coulter. Both men feel that a 50:50

partnership would be unworkable, but have agreed to consider the following two options:

(1) Outright purchase of 100% of the share capital of FOCUS by HARRINGTON for a consideration of €4,000,000. This would be financed by:

   (i)   The issue of 500,000 shares in HARRINGTON at a price of €6.00 per share (nominal value = €1.00); and

   (ii) €1,000,000 from HARRINGTON's cash resources.

(2) Purchase of an 18% stake in FOCUS by HARRINGTON for €850,000 cash. Patrick Harrington would join the existing two directors on the Board of FOCUS and monthly Board meetings would be held to agree the strategic direction of the company. The three directors would have equal voting power.

Requirements:

Issue (a)

 (i) In relation to the potential new car dealership, explain the correct accounting treatment of the inventory with reference to relevant international accounting standards.

(ii) Set out the journals required to reflect your recommended accounting treatment under (a), together with the relevant disclosures.

6 Marks

Issue (b)

 (i) Advise Patrick as to the recommended accounting treatment and disclosure of the vacant leased premises, setting out journals as appropriate.

(ii) Set out the costs that may be capitalised in the accounts in relation to the new building, and any relevant adjusting journal.

(iii) Set out the journals required to incorporate the correct valuation into the financial statements, together with any relevant disclosures and requirements.

18 Marks

Issue (c)

(i) Advise Patrick regarding the possibility of capitalising the costs incurred in relation to the installation of the new machinery. Provide relevant journals and disclosures.

4 Marks

Issue (d)

(i) Advise Patrick as to the accounting treatment and disclosure of the cars held for rental under the proposed contract hire arrangement.

4 Marks

Issue (e)

(i) Explain to Patrick how each of the two options for investment in FOCUS would appear in the separate financial statements of HARRINGTON for the year ended 31 December 2x06. Provide journals for each scenario, incorporating the investment in the financial statements, and advice as to the necessary disclosures.

8 Marks

(ii) Regarding the proposed investment in FOCUS on 30 June 2x06, explain, using journals, the accounting treatment of each of the options in the consolidated accounts of HARRINGTON for the year ended 31 December 2x06.

10 Marks

Total 50 Marks

NB Re-drafted financial statements and consolidated financial statements are NOT required.

Ignore any taxation implications of recommended accounting adjustments.

It should be noted that, in their separate financial statements, all companies within the group account at cost for investments in subsidiaries, joint ventures and associates.

Appendix I

Focus Ltd
Statement of Comprehensive Income
For the Year Ended 30 June 2x06

	€
Revenue	6,235,367
Cost of sales	(3,990,635)
Gross profit	2,244,732
Administrative expenses	(1,425,235)
Finance costs	(66,538)
Profit before tax	752,959
Income tax expense	(185,235)
Profit for the year	567,724

Statement of Financial Position as at 30 June 2x06

	€
Assets	
Non-current assets	
- Premises, plant and equipment	2,542,698
Current assets	1,482,615
	4,025,313
Equity and liabilities	
Capital and reserves	
- Share capital	500,000
- Retained earnings	2,371,692
Total equity	2,871,692
Non-current liabilities	175,500
Current liabilities	978,121
Total equity and liabilities	4,025,313

THE O'NEILL GROUP*

Introduction

The O'Neill Group of companies is a successful wholesale and retail group. The owner, Mr David O'Neill, took over his father's department store several years ago, updated its image, restored its profitability and developed the business to its current status. In 2x00, Mr O'Neill decided to open an in-store restaurant for shoppers and other passing trade. The restaurant business (an incorporated entity) has proved to be a more difficult area for the group due to changing trends and the performance of this company has been inconsistent over the years. The wholesale business, on the other hand, has developed in tandem with the retail outlet and has a steady trade with an established customer base. The group structure is straightforward, with O'Neill Enterprises Ltd ('O'Neill Enterprises') owning 100% of O'Neill Retail Ltd ('O'Neill Retail') and O'Neill Wholesale Ltd ('O'Neill Wholesale'), and 60% of O'Neill Restaurant Ltd ('O'Neill Restaurant').

Mr O'Neill is keen to further advance the business by making some changes in the group structure and would like your advice on the following issues in the form of a report. The accounting issues and relevant financial information are set out in **Appendix I** and **II** respectively.

*2005 Paper 2(i) in the Final Admitting Examination of the Institute of Chartered Accountants in Ireland

Requirements:

Issue 1

Advise Mr O'Neill as to the recommended accounting treatment relating to the new refund policy of O'Neill Retail, setting out any journals required and all relevant disclosures relating to the financial statements for the year ended 31 December 2x05.

7 Marks

Issue 2

(a) Set out how the part-disposal of O'Neill Restaurant will impact on the financial statements of O'Neill Enterprises for the year ended 31 December 2x05 under international accounting standards. Provide relevant journals.

3 Marks

(b) Explain how the part disposal of O'Neill Restaurant will be reflected in the consolidated financial statements of the group for the year ended 31 December 2x05 under international accounting standards, providing relevant journals and disclosures.

8 Marks

(c) Explain to Mr O'Neill, with reference to relevant international accounting standards, how O'Neill Restaurant will be treated in the group financial statements from 1 January 2x06.

11 Marks

Issue 3

(a) For each of the areas outlined under Issue 3 of **Appendix I**, compare the accounting policies adopted by Reid Enterprises and O'Neill Wholesale. Advise Mr O'Neill as to whether the policies of Reid Enterprises are in line with international accounting standards.

9 Marks

(b) Compute the goodwill arising on the purchase of Reid Enterprises, based on the information available, and discuss the accounting treatment under international accounting standards.

6 Marks

(c) Set out the journals that will be required to incorporate the trade, assets and liabilities of Reid Enterprises into O'Neill Wholesale on 1 January 2x06 under international accounting standards. Advise Mr O'Neill as to any disclosures required in the financial statements of O'Neill Wholesale for the year ended 31 December 2x05.

6 Marks

Total 50 Marks

NB Re-drafted financial statements and consolidated financial statements are not required.

It should be noted that, in their separate/individual financial statements, all companies within the group account at cost for investments in subsidiaries, joint ventures and associates.

It is group policy to measure any non-controlling interest in subsidiaries at the non-controlling interest's proportionate share of the acquired company's identifiable net assets.

Appendix I

Issue 1 – O'Neill Retail

O'Neill Retail has introduced a new policy in 2x05 of refunding purchases by dissatisfied customers if goods are returned within one month with a proof of purchase. This facility is now well known among the customer base and has proved popular with customers, prompting an increase in sales. It is anticipated that approximately 5% of goods will be returned. The sales for December 2x05 were €550,000 with the average margin being 20%. Mr O'Neill would like to know the correct accounting treatment and necessary disclosures for the new refunds policy.

Issue 2 – Part-disposal of O'Neill Restaurant

O'Neill Restaurant was incorporated seven years ago, funded by an investment in share capital by O'Neill Enterprises of €10,000. In its initial few years, the company traded well and built up an established clientele. However, it then entered a period of decline and its turnover and profitability suffered. A new restaurant manager was recruited four years ago, and he has worked very hard since then to develop the customer base and to increase the turnover and profitability of the company.

In 2x04, he was headhunted by a competitor and, in a bid to keep him in situ, Mr O'Neill offered him an opportunity to purchase a stake in the company. At 31 December 2x04, the manager purchased 40% of the company at a price of €200,000. He is keen to purchase a further 30% of the company and a consideration of €175,000 has been negotiated with a completion date of 31 December 2x05. Mr O'Neill intends to retain the remaining 30% as he still wishes to continue his active involvement in the running of the restaurant and will still contribute to the management of the operation. No entries relating to the 30% purchase have been reflected in the Statement of Financial Position (page 169).

The fair value of the remaining investment in O'Neill Restaurant (i.e. 30%) at 31 December 2x05 was €154,000.

Mr O'Neill would like to understand the impact of this further sale on the financial statements of O'Neill Enterprises and on the consolidated financial statements for the year ended 31 December 2x05. He would also like to know how O'Neill Restaurant will be treated in the consolidated financial statements for the year ended 31 December 2x06.

Issue 3 – Potential acquisition of Reid Enterprises Ltd

O'Neill Wholesale is in negotiations to acquire the trade and net assets of a competitor, Reid Enterprises Ltd ('Reid Enterprises'). There are some differences in accounting policies between the two companies and Mr O'Neill would like to understand the main differences and their effect on the financial statements. He would also welcome comments on whether the policies of Reid Enterprises are in line with international accounting standards. The key areas meriting consideration are as follows:

Valuation of property
O'Neill Wholesale includes its non-specialised warehouse in its financial statements based on its depreciated cost and discloses the open market value of the premises in the financial statements. Reid Enterprises, however, incorporates the market value of its premises into the financial statements. The market value of the premises owned by Reid Enterprises is €600,000 higher than the existing use value as there is a strong possibility of rezoning of the area in the future. The property owned by Reid Enterprises will be disposed of post-acquisition and new premises acquired to house the operation.

Furthermore, the financial statements of Reid Enterprises **(Appendix II)** include a deferred tax liability of €200,000 relating to the temporary difference created by the revaluation of the asset. Reid Enterprises has not yet entered into an agreement with a third party for sale of the premises.

Related party note
Mr O'Neill is aware that Reid Enterprises has several transactions with related companies, and the significance of these transactions is set out in the notes to the financial statements. He has noticed, however, that the names of the transacting companies have not been disclosed.

Acquisition of trade, assets and liabilities

It has been agreed in principle that the acquisition will take place as from 1 January 2x06. Only the trade, assets and liabilities of Reid Enterprises will be purchased and the calculation of the goodwill will follow the guidance for acquisition accounting under international accounting standards, with the consideration being €2,000,000 payable in cash by O'Neill Wholesale.

Appendix II

O'Neill Restaurant Ltd

Statement of Comprehensive Income for the Year Ended 31 December

	2x05	2x04
	€	€
Revenue	250,000	225,000
Cost of sales	(175,000)	(162,000)
Gross profit	75,000	63,000
Administrative expenses	(20,000)	(18,000)
Profit before tax	55,000	45,000
Income tax expense	(5,000)	–
Profit for the period	50,000	45,000

O'Neill Restaurant Ltd
Statement of Financial Position as at 31 December

	2x05	2x04
	€	€
Assets		
Non-current assets		
Property, plant and equipment	65,000	68,000
Current assets	80,000	60,000
Inter-company receivables	43,000	12,000
	188,000	140,000
Equity and liabilities		
Share capital	10,000	10,000
Retained earnings	146,000	96,000
	156,000	106,000
Current liabilities	32,000	34,000
Total equity and liabilities	188,000	140,000

The fair value of the net identifiable assets of O'Neill Restaurant at 31 December 2x05 was €180,000.

Reid Enterprises Ltd
Statement of Financial Position as at 31 December

	2x05 €	2x04 €
Assets		
Non-current assets		
Property, plant and equipment	2,100,000	2,203,000
Current assets	2,350,000	2,000,000
	4,450,000	4,203,000
Equity and liabilities		
Share capital	100,000	100,000
Reserves	749,850	458,000
	849,850	558,000
Non-current liabilities		
Long-term liabilities	1,100,000	1,300,000
Provisions	400,000	395,000
Current liabilities	2,100,150	1,950,000
Total equity and liabilities	4,450,000	4,203,000

FITZWILLIAM GROUP*

Introduction

FITZWILLIAM GROUP Ltd ('FITZWILLIAM GROUP') is a holding company and has 100% stake in each of the following companies. It is the policy of all group companies to prepare financial statements under international accounting standards.

FITZWILLIAM CONSTRUCTION Ltd ('FITZWILLIAM CONSTRUCTION') is a company whose principal activity is the construction of buildings on behalf of third parties. FITZWILLIAM CONSTRUCTION also acts as the principal contractor on development projects for buildings purchased by FITZWILLIAM RENTAL Ltd ('FITZWILLIAM RENTAL'). FITZWILLIAM RENTAL is a property investment company which holds property for rental and also owns the group headquarters building. FITZWILLIAM RENTAL uses the fair value model when dealing with investment property and the revaluation model under IAS for all other completed properties. FITZWILLIAM RETAIL Ltd ('FITZWILLIAM RETAIL') is a company which owns several department stores. FITZWILLIAM GROUP acts as a management company and is the entity through which the directors are remunerated.

*2006 Paper 2(i) in the Final Admitting Examination of the Institute of Chartered Accountants in Ireland

DIAGRAM OF GROUP

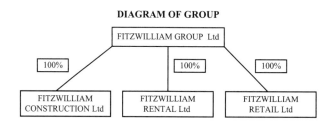

Various accounting issues have arisen within the group companies, and the Financial Controller has asked for your advice on a range of accounting issues which should be provided in the form of a memorandum. These issues are set out below.

(a) Fitzwilliam Construction

On 1 January 2x05 this company entered into a contract to develop a building for a third party. The contract sum was €1,700,000 and the building work is well under way, with costs incurred to date of €920,000. The project has now run into difficulties and the project manager estimates that the costs to completion will be a further €850,000. In addition, the building work on site has caused some contamination to the surrounding environment with an expected clean up cost of €200,000. FITZWILLIAM CONSTRUCTION has a widely published environmental policy in which it makes good all contamination that it causes and has a record of honouring this published policy.

(b) Fitzwilliam Rental

FITZWILLIAM RENTAL purchased a disused building in the city docklands at a cost of €1,500,000 on 1 January 2x05. The intention at this time was to develop the property and to subsequently let the various floors to professional firms. A further €300,000 was spent over the next 11 months on renovations and improvements to the building prior to letting, with €200,000 of this being for work done at cost by FITZWILLIAM CONSTRUCTION. The building was ready for tenant occupation on 1 December 2x05. The valuation of the completed property at 31 December 2x05 was €2,000,000. Due to unforeseen difficulties in obtaining tenants, the building remained unoccupied.

In February 2x06, the docklands property was valued at €2,100,000 and the group then decided to immediately relocate its headquarters to this building. FITZWILLIAM RENTAL managed to secure new tenants for the group's 'old' headquarters. The book value of those headquarters was €1,500,000 and the market value at the date of letting in February 2x06 was €1,800,000. The valuations of both properties were provided by independent qualified valuers. The Financial Controller would like your advice as to how to account for these property movements under international accounting standards.

Heating system in new headquarters

The group moved into the new docklands property in February 2x06. The property has an estimated life of 50 years. However, it contains a sophisticated air conditioning and heating system at a cost of €200,000 which is included in the value of the building of €2,100,000. The heating system will require replacement every 10 years and the company has entered into a contract with its supplier to replace the heating system at an agreed price of €200,000 every 10 years. The company plans to depreciate the building at €42,000 per annum and provide a further €20,000 each year to facilitate the replacement of the heating system. The policy of FITZWILLIAM RENTAL is to depreciate assets on a monthly basis, and not to depreciate in the month of addition.

(c)   **Fitzwilliam Retail**

FITZWILLIAM RETAIL entered into a transaction in March 2x05 whereby it agreed to enter into a sale of one of its department stores to a third party in order to raise capital for another project. At that time FITZWILLIAM RETAIL also entered into a 10-year operating lease to lease back the store at a market rental. The sale price of the store was set at its market value of €2,500,000 and the book value of the property in the books of FITZWIL-LIAM RETAIL prior to the sale was €2,200,000.

(d)   **Fitzwilliam Group**

As the group has had a profitable trading year, the Board, at its meeting on 14 January 2x06, decided to propose a dividend of €750,000 in respect of the year ended 31 December 2x05. In addition, the Board agreed that, during the year ending 31 December 2x06, it would grant 50 share options to each of its 100 employees with a commencement date of 1 January 2x06. Each grant is conditional on the employee working for the group for the next four years. The fair value of each share option at 1 January 2x06 was €20. It is likely that 25% of employees will leave during the four-year period, and thus forfeit their rights under the share option scheme. It is assumed that these departures will occur evenly over the four-year period.

Requirements:

Issue (a) – Fitzwilliam Construction

Advise the company as to the correct accounting treatment and disclosure for the contract under consideration with reference to relevant international accounting standards, together with supporting journals.

13 Marks

Issue (b) – Fitzwilliam Rental

(i) Explain, with reference to international accounting standards, the accounting treatment which should be applied to the docklands property in the financial statements of FITZWILLIAM RENTAL for the year ended 31 December 2x05. Journals are **not** required.

9 Marks

(ii) Provide details of the relevant accounting treatment and disclosure in the financial statements of FITZWILLIAM RENTAL for the year ending 31 December 2x06 for the docklands property and also for the old group headquarters. Journals are **not** required.

6 Marks

(iii) Advise the Financial Controller, with reference to relevant international accounting standards, as to the correct accounting treatment for the air conditioning and heating system in the financial statements of FITZWILLIAM RENTAL for the year ending 31 December 2x06. Journals are **not** required.

5 Marks

Issue (c) – Fitzwilliam Retail

Explain with reference to international accounting standards, the accounting treatment of the property transaction undertaken in the year ended 31 December 2x05 in the books of FITZWILLIAM RETAIL. Provide relevant journals to reflect this transaction. Disclosures are **not** required.

6 Marks

Issue (d) – Fitzwilliam Group

(i) Explain, with reference to international accounting standards, how the proposed dividend will be reflected in the financial statements for the year ended 31 December 2x05.

4 Marks

(ii) Advise the Financial Controller on how the share options will be reflected in the financial statements for the year ending 31 December 2x06, together with details of disclosures required by international accounting standards.

7 Marks

Total 50 Marks

NB Ignore all taxation implications.

HARDING GROUP*

Introduction

HARDING plc ('HARDING') is the holding company of a group of companies which prepares consolidated financial statements in accordance with international accounting standards. The principal activities of HARDING are as a holding company and also as a property investment company. Throughout the year ended 31 December 2x06 the holding company owned 100% of two subsidiaries which are listed below:

GOLF plc ('GOLF')   A company whose principal activity is the sale of books through an internet website. The company has been underperforming in recent years and the sale of the company is currently being negotiated.

HOLLY plc ('HOLLY')   A company specialising in research and development in the chemical industry which was acquired during the year ended 31 December 2x05.

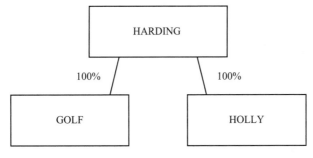

*2007 Paper 2(i) in the Final Admitting Examination of the Institute of Chartered Accountants in Ireland

A further acquisition, PROSPECT plc ('PROSPECT'), is also being considered by the Board of Directors of HARDING.

The Group Financial Director has approached you for advice in relation to various issues affecting the consolidated financial statements for the year ended 31 December 2x06 and he would like you to prepare a memorandum dealing with the matters listed below.

Requirements:

Prepare the memorandum for the Group Financial Director covering the following matters in respect of the year ended 31 December 2x06:

(a) (i) Advise the Group Financial Director as to the appropriateness of the costs included in 'Other operating expenses' in GOLF with reference to relevant international accounting standards.

5 Marks

(ii) Explain how GOLF will be shown in the consolidated financial statements with reference to relevant international accounting standards. Disclosures are **not** required.

12 Marks

(b) Advise the Group Financial Director as to the correct accounting treatment of the head office property and the investment property held in HARDING. Provide relevant journals, ignoring any impact on the depreciation charge.

8 Marks

(c) (i) Set out the correct accounting treatment to reflect the final net asset valuation of HOLLY, with reference to relevant international accounting standards. Journals are **not** required.

8 Marks

(ii) Advise the Group Financial Director as to the correct accounting treatment of the development costs incurred in the years ended 31 December 2x05 and 31 December 2x06, with reference to relevant international accounting standards. Journals and disclosures are **not** required.

10 Marks

(d) Explain the correct accounting treatment of the deferred tax issues in PROSPECT, and set out any relevant journals. Disclosures are **not** required.

7 Marks

Total 50 Marks

NB Ignore all taxation implications other than in relation to Requirement (d).

It should be noted that, in their separate/individual financial statements, all companies within the group account at cost for investments in subsidiaries, jointly controlled entities and associates.

Golf plc

GOLF has been a loss-making subsidiary for many years and the Board agreed at a Board meeting in November 2x06 to sell GOLF to a third party as a going concern. A price has been agreed, and final negotiations are currently under way with an anticipated completion date of September 2x07. Employees and customers were informed in December 2x06 of the pending sale. The Group Financial Director is keen to exclude GOLF from the consolidated financial statements for the year ended 31 December 2x06 on the grounds that it is no longer part of continuing group operations due to its impending sale. In previous years, GOLF was included in the group results. Summary financial information for GOLF is included below:

Golf plc – Statement of Comprehensive Income

	2x06 € million	2x05 € million
Turnover	80	50
Cost of sales	(50)	(70)
Gross profit/loss	30	(20)
Other operating expenses	(140)	(30)
Loss before tax	(110)	(50)

Included within 'Other operating expenses' in the financial statements of GOLF for the year ended 31 December 2x06 were the following:

	€ million
Operating costs incurred	92
Provision for future operating losses	30
Impairment of assets	18
	140

The Group Financial Director would like to gain a fuller understanding of how the results of GOLF will be shown in the consolidated financial statements for the year ended 31 December 2x06.

Harding plc

HARDING owns two properties. One is used as the company's head office and is included in 'Property, plant and equipment' and the other is an investment property that is leased to a third party on a 10-year operating lease. In the past, HARDING has revalued the head office building each year and transferred any movement to the revaluation reserve. The investment property was purchased during the year ended 31 December 2x05.

Relevant details of the cost and fair values of the properties are as follows:

	Head Office € million	Investment Property € million
Cost	20	19
Valuation 31 December 2x05	31	n/a
Valuation 31 December 2x06	29	23

The valuations at 31 December 2x06 have not yet been incorporated into the financial statements. The Board would like to apply the fair value model to its investment property for the current reporting period. Ignore any depreciation impact.

Holly plc

On 1 March 2x05 the group acquired a subsidiary company, HOLLY, for a consideration of €10 million. At the time of completion of the 2x05 financial statements, a final valuation of net assets was not available, and goodwill was provisionally based on a net asset value of €8 million. The final valuation became available in December 2x06 and shows a net asset value of €7 million. The Group Financial Director has asked you to advise as to the effect of this information on the consolidated financial statements for the year ended 31 December 2x06.

HOLLY is currently engaged in a research and development project to develop a new chemical. The development costs in the year ended 31 December 2x05 of €5 million were written off, as the management felt they were not sufficiently confident of the ultimate profitability of the project. In the year ended 31 December 2x06 further development costs of €10 million have been incurred, with only an estimated €200,000 of costs to be incurred in the future. Production is expected to commence in the next few months.

The total trading profits from sales of the new product are now estimated at €20 million and the Board has decided to complete the project. The directors have again decided to write off the costs incurred in the year ended 31 December 2x06. The Group Financial Director has asked for your advice on whether this accounting treatment is in line with international accounting standards.

Prospect plc

The group is currently considering a further acquisition, PROSPECT, a property investment company. The Financial Director has been reviewing the group deferred taxation provision and would like your advice on the impact of the following:

(1) PROSPECT has a portfolio of readily marketable government securities which are held as current assets at market value in the statement of financial position, with any increase or decrease being taken to the statement of comprehensive income. The gains on these investments are taxed when the investments are sold, and at present the securities are valued at €5 million above cost.

(2) PROSPECT intends to make an additional accrual for pension contributions of €1 million. This will not be allowable for tax purposes until it is paid.

Assume a Corporation Tax rate of 30%.

DARCY GROUP*

Introduction

DARCY plc ('DARCY') is the holding company of a group of companies which prepares individual and consolidated financial statements in accordance with international accounting standards (IFRS/IAS).

The principal activity of DARCY is as a holding company and throughout the year ended 31 December 2x07 DARCY owned 100% of BINGLEY plc ('BINGLEY') and BENNETT plc ('BENNETT').

BINGLEY is a company whose principal activity is commercial and residential property development. The company has been very profitable in recent years and its Board of Directors is hoping to expand the company further by forming relationships with similar companies.

BENNETT is a company whose principal activity is the wholesale distribution of timber and other building supplies, some of which are also manufactured by the company.

Diagram of Group Structure

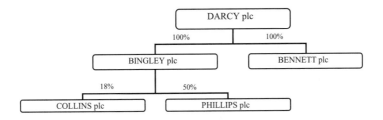

The Financial Director of the group, Mr Fitzwilliam, has approached you for advice in relation to various issues which will affect the individual and consolidated

* 2008 Paper 2(i) in the Final Admitting Examination of the Institute of Chartered Accountants in Ireland

financial statements of the group for the year ended 31 December 2x07. He would like you to prepare a memorandum for him advising on how the matters detailed below should be treated.

It should be noted that, in their separate/individual financial statements, all companies within the group account at cost for investments in subsidiaries, jointly controlled entities and associates.

It is group policy to measure any non-controlling interest in subsidiaries at the non-controlling interest's proportionate share of the acquired company's identifiable net assets.

Bingley plc

Transactions with Collins plc

BINGLEY holds an 18% interest in another property development company, COLLINS. COLLINS has several other corporate shareholders. The majority of its shares are held by a property investment company unconnected with the DARCY group. BINGLEY is represented on the Board of Directors of COLLINS and, via this representation, participates in all major decisions required to be taken in the management of the company. BINGLEY regularly supplies COLLINS with development land and, during the year ended 31 December 2x07, BINGLEY sold a development site to COLLINS at its open market value of €2,000,000. BINGLEY had purchased the site during the same year for €1,800,000.

Transactions with Phillips plc

During the year ended 31 December 2x07, BINGLEY entered into a contract with an unconnected property development company under which a new company, PHILLIPS, was formed. BINGLEY owns 50% of the shares in PHILLIPS, with the other 50% being held by the other party to the agreement. PHILLIPS was formed for the purpose of undertaking a major commercial property development project, which neither of its shareholders could undertake alone due to its size and the working capital investment required. The two companies therefore decided to undertake the project jointly via a new company. The contractual arrangement between the two shareholders is such that PHILLIPS will be managed by them jointly for the duration of the development project, and all profits or losses will be divided equally between them once the project is complete. It is anticipated that the project will take 2 to 3 years to complete.

BINGLEY wishes to account for this contract in accordance with international accounting standards (IAS/IFRS).

Bennett plc

Acquisition of Industrial Saw

On 1 January 2x07 BENNETT acquired an industrial saw from AB Finance Ltd on a finance lease. The lease payments are €5,000 per annum for four years with an option to extend payments for a further two years at €500 per annum. The first payment was made upon delivery and subsequent payments are made annually in advance. The interest rate implicit in the lease is 12% per annum and the machine will have an estimated life of four years.

Shipment of Timber Products

On 19 December 2x07, BENNETT delivered a large shipment of timber products to a potential new customer. BENNETT had agreed with the customer that the goods would be sent subject to the customer's approval and could be returned, without cost to the customer, within 10 days of delivery. The customer agreed to speak with BENNETT's sales representative within the 10-day period to advise him of whether the goods met with approval or not. The customer had not, however, contacted the company by the year-end of 31 December 2x07. The sales value of the shipment was €220,000 and this has not been included in the revenue of BENNETT for the year.

Inventories

BENNETT's inventories of building supplies include a great number of small products that cannot be specifically identified. Such items, referred to as "Category C" inventories, have always been included in the financial statements of the company on a last-in, first-out (LIFO) basis. These inventories are valued at €640,000 at 31 December 2x07.

Mr Fitzwilliam had been content with this method of valuation of the inventories for a number of years, as the cost of the products did not tend to move significantly. However, in the current year (year ended 31 December 2x07), he has noted that the cost of some products has decreased considerably, with the effect that the inventories would be valued at €530,000 if a first-in, first-out (FIFO) basis of valuation were used.

Mr Fitzwilliam has also noted that other inventories, included in the draft financial statements of BENNETTT for the year ended 31 December 2x07 at a value of €130,000, could currently be sold for €280,000 as the product has become very popular with consumers. These inventories originally cost €190,000, but had been written down to €130,000 at 31 December 2x06.

Grant Assistance

During the year ended 31 December 2x07, BENNETT received a government grant to partially finance the purchase of some items of plant and machinery required for a planned expansion of the manufacturing side of the business. Expenditure of up to €1,500,000 of plant and machinery was approved by the government department involved, with the grant being approved for 60% of the total expenditure. The full amount of the grant had been received by 31 December 2x07.

The conditions on which the grant was approved were that the expenditure would relate to the purchase of specific items of plant and machinery and that an additional 10 members of staff would be hired.

At 31 December 2x07, BENNETT had hired 12 extra staff members and had purchased €1,200,000 of the specified plant and machinery. It is the intention of the directors, if cash flow permits, to purchase a further €600,000 worth of plant and machinery in the year ended 31 December 2x08.

The plant and machinery purchased will be depreciated at 8% per annum on a straight-line basis. It is the company's policy to depreciate assets fully in the year of acquisition, regardless of the date of purchase.

The directors of BENNETT feel that it is important to show grant assistance received separately in the financial statements. To date, the only accounting entry in relation to the grant received has been to record it as a separate item within deferred income in the draft financial statements of the company for the year.

Requirements:

(a) Bingley plc

    (i) Advise Mr Fitzwilliam as to the correct accounting treatment and disclosure of the interest in COLLINS, and the sale of land to that company, in the consolidated financial statements of the DARCY group for the year ended 31 December 2x07, with reference to international accounting standards (IAS/IFRS). Journals are **not** required.

14 Marks

(ii) Explain, with reference to international accounting standards (IAS/IFRS), how the interest in PHILLIPS should be accounted for in the consolidated financial statements of DARCY. Journals and disclosure notes are **not** required.

6 Marks

(b) Bennett plc

(i) Advise Mr Fitzwilliam, with reference to international accounting standards (IAS/IFRS), of the correct accounting treatment of the finance lease in the financial statements of BENNETT for the year ended 31 December 2x07. Show the relevant extracts in the statement of comprehensive income and statement of financial position. Disclosure notes are **not** required.

8 Marks

(ii) Explain, with reference to international accounting standards (IAS/IFRS) the correct accounting treatment, together with supporting journals, of the shipment of timber products delivered to the potential new customer on 19 December 2x07 in the financial statements of BENNETT for the year ended 31 December 2x07. Disclosure notes are **not** required.

4 Marks

(iii) Advise Mr Fitzwilliam of the correct accounting treatment, under international accounting standards (IAS/IFRS) of the issues relating to the company's inventories in the financial statements of the company for the year ended 31 December 2x07. Set out any relevant journals. Disclosure notes are **not** required.

10 Marks

(iv) Explain, with reference to international accounting standards (IAS/IFRS), the correct accounting treatment, including any relevant journals, of the government grant received by the company in the financial statements for the year ended 31 December 2x07. Draft the disclosure notes required.

8 Marks
Total 50 Marks

Present Value Table

Present value of 1, i.e. $(1 + r)^{-n}$
where r = discount rate
n = number of periods until payment

Discount rates (r)

Periods (n)	1%	2%	3%	4%	5%	6%	7%	8%	9%	10%
1	0.990	0.980	0.971	0.962	0.952	0.943	0.935	0.926	0.917	0.909
2	0.980	0.961	0.943	0.925	0.907	0.890	0.873	0.857	0.842	0.826
3	0.971	0.942	0.915	0.889	0.864	0.840	0.816	0.794	0.772	0.751
4	0.961	0.924	0.888	0.855	0.823	0.792	0.763	0.735	0.708	0.683
5	0.951	0.906	0.863	0.822	0.784	0.747	0.713	0.681	0.650	0.621
6	0.942	0.888	0.837	0.790	0.746	0.705	0.666	0.630	0.596	0.564
7	0.933	0.871	0.813	0.760	0.711	0.665	0.623	0.583	0.547	0.513
8	0.923	0.853	0.789	0.731	0.677	0.627	0.582	0.540	0.502	0.467
9	0.914	0.837	0.766	0.703	0.645	0.592	0.544	0.500	0.460	0.424
10	0.905	0.820	0.744	0.676	0.614	0.558	0.508	0.463	0.422	0.386
11	0.896	0.804	0.722	0.650	0.585	0.527	0.475	0.429	0.388	0.350
12	0.887	0.788	0.701	0.625	0.557	0.497	0.444	0.397	0.356	0.319
13	0.879	0.773	0.681	0.601	0.530	0.469	0.415	0.368	0.326	0.290
14	0.870	0.758	0.661	0.577	0.505	0.442	0.388	0.340	0.299	0.263
15	0.861	0.743	0.642	0.555	0.481	0.417	0.362	0.315	0.275	0.239

	11%	12%	13%	14%	15%	16%	17%	18%	19%	20%
1	0.901	0.893	0.885	0.877	0.870	0.862	0.855	0.847	0.840	0.833
2	0.812	0.797	0.783	0.769	0.756	0.743	0.731	0.718	0.706	0.694
3	0.731	0.712	0.693	0.675	0.658	0.641	0.624	0.609	0.593	0.579
4	0.659	0.636	0.613	0.592	0.572	0.552	0.534	0.516	0.499	0.482
5	0.593	0.567	0.543	0.519	0.497	0.476	0.456	0.437	0.419	0.402
6	0.535	0.507	0.480	0.456	0.432	0.410	0.390	0.370	0.352	0.335
7	0.482	0.452	0.425	0.400	0.376	0.354	0.333	0.314	0.296	0.279
8	0.434	0.404	0.376	0.351	0.327	0.305	0.285	0.266	0.249	0.233
9	0.391	0.361	0.333	0.308	0.284	0.263	0.243	0.225	0.209	0.194
10	0.352	0.322	0.295	0.270	0.247	0.227	0.208	0.191	0.176	0.162
11	0.317	0.287	0.261	0.237	0.215	0.195	0.178	0.162	0.148	0.135
12	0.286	0.257	0.231	0.208	0.187	0.168	0.152	0.137	0.124	0.112
13	0.258	0.229	0.204	0.182	0.163	0.145	0.130	0.116	0.104	0.093
14	0.232	0.205	0.181	0.160	0.141	0.125	0.111	0.099	0.088	0.078
15	0.209	0.183	0.160	0.140	0.123	0.108	0.095	0.084	0.074	0.065

ROCKET GROUP

Introduction

ROCKET plc ('ROCKET') is the holding company of a group of companies which prepares their financial statements in accordance with international accounting standards. The principal activity of ROCKET is to act as a holding company. Throughout the year ended 31 December 2x07 the holding company owned 100% of two subsidiaries which are listed below:

LAUNCH plc ('LAUNCH')   A company whose principal activity is the manufacture and sale of carpets to retail outlets.

SPACE plc ('SPACE')   A company specialising in developing and promoting a range of bathroom accessories.

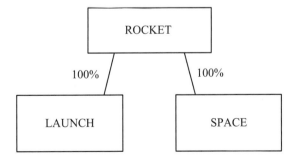

The Group Financial Director has approached you for advice in relation to various issues affecting the consolidated financial statements for the year ended 31 December 2x07 and she would like you to prepare a memorandum dealing with the matters listed below.

Requirements:

Prepare the memorandum for the Group Financial Director covering the following matters in respect of the year ended 31 December 2x07:

(a) **(i)** Advise the Group Financial Director as to the accounting treatment of the work in progress inventory of LAUNCH at 31 December 2x07. Your advice should be based on the specialised carpet inventory only, and should take no account of the sale of surplus carpet materials in (a) (ii) below. Disclosures are **not** required.

14 Marks

(ii) Explain how LAUNCH should account for the surplus carpet materials, with reference to relevant international accounting standards. Provide relevant journals. Disclosures are **not** required.

5 Marks

(iii) Advise the Group Financial Director as to the correct accounting treatment of the wool inventory of LAUNCH at 31 December 2x07. Provide relevant journals. Disclosures are **not** required.

5 Marks

(iv) Set out the correct accounting treatment in respect of the sale and lease-back of the factory and car park of LAUNCH. Provide relevant journals. Disclosures are **not** required.

14 marks

(b) **(i)** Advise the Group Financial Director regarding the correct accounting treatment of the purchase and disposal of the building by SPACE. Provide relevant journals **and** disclosures.

12 marks

Total 50 Marks

NB   **Ignore all taxation implications.**

It should be noted that, in their separate/individual financial statements, all companies within the group account at cost for investments in subsidiaries, joint ventures and associates.

Launch plc

(i) Work in progress inventory

LAUNCH manufactures a range of specially designed carpets for the hotel and leisure industry, and a custom built factory was constructed for this purpose. LAUNCH has achieved its target output of 10,000 customised carpets in each of the years 2x03–2x06. During 2x07, this production level was exceeded however, due to staff agreeing to work double shifts in order to meet an unexpected increase in demand during the summer season. Consequently, 12,000 finished carpets were produced in the year ended 31 December 2x07.

At 31 December 2x07, LAUNCH had 200 carpets in inventory, which on average were 75% complete. Each completed carpet incurs the following costs:

	€
Materials	1,500
Labour	600
Distribution costs	100
Sales commissions	150
	2,350

The following additional costs were incurred in the year ended 31 December 2x07, in respect of the overall operation of the factory:

	€
Production supervisors' salaries	2,550,000
Depreciation of equipment	1,250,000
Administration costs	400,000
Interest relating to financing of inventory	90,000

One of the above 75% completed carpets was manufactured for the Regency, a family-run hotel, which, after a poor winter season, decided to close with immediate effect in early January 2x08. The general manager of the factory is confident that, if LAUNCH spends a total of €800 on promotion and distribution costs, the carpet can be offloaded to another hotel group for €3,000.

(ii) Carpet ends and floor mats

During 2x07, LAUNCH decided to market surplus carpet materials as carpet ends and floor mats. Previously, these materials had been dumped, but with spiralling waste disposal costs, it was decided to opt for an alternative use approach.

During 2x07, a cash surplus of €130,000 was generated from the sale of these products, and it was estimated that inventories of surplus carpet materials at 31 December 2x07 could be sold in January for further net proceeds of €25,000.

(iii) Inventory of Wool

Wool is the primary material used by LAUNCH for the manufacture of specialised carpets. Wool inventory at 31 December 2x07 had cost €600,000 to purchase, but only had a net realisable value of €200,000. On the basis that LAUNCH does not intend to dispose of the wool, the inventory has been included in the financial statements at a value of €450,000. It is believed that this partially reflects the fall in value of the wool, but also takes account of the intention to retain the inventory for use in the production process. It is expected that the finished carpets, into which the wool will be incorporated, can be sold at a reasonable profit margin.

(iv) Sale and Leaseback

On the 1 January 2x07, the factory that is used for the manufacture of specialised carpets, along with its three-acre car park, was sold to an insurance company. Both assets were immediately leased back to LAUNCH under a 50-year lease agreement.

The factory, which was completed in 2x02, had cost €6 million to construct. The car park had been purchased and developed alongside, at an additional cost of €4 million. Up to the time of their sale, both assets had been carried in the financial statements using the revaluation model of IAS 16. On the 31 December 2x06, the factory was included in the financial statements of LAUNCH at its fair value of €10 million. The parking lot was included in the statement of financial position at €7 million on the same date.

Under the terms of the sale and leaseback agreement of 1 January 2x07, the factory was sold to the insurance company for €12 million, and the consideration agreed for the car park was €9 million, which was its fair value at the time of sale.

LAUNCH agreed to pay 50 annual instalments, in advance, of €500,000 in respect of the factory. LAUNCH has an option to extend the lease of the factory for a secondary period of 25 years by making further annual payments of €10,000.

LAUNCH agreed to pay 50 annual instalments, in advance, of €400,000 in respect of the lease of the car park.

LAUNCH charges depreciation of 2% per annum straight line on the factory, and no depreciation is charged in respect of the car park. Interest on finance leases is charged on a straight line basis over the primary lease term, as it is believed that this provides a reasonable approximation in this case of a constant periodic rate of interest.

Space plc

Building

On 1 January 2x03, SPACE purchased a building for €6 million. The building was depreciated over 50 years on a straight line basis. A full year's depreciation is charged in the year of purchase, and no depreciation is charged in the year of sale.

On 1 January 2x05, the building was deemed to have suffered an impairment, and it was written down to €4 million. On 1 January 2x07, the building was revalued to €7 million. It was sold to LAUNCH on 31 December 2x07 for €8 million, which was certified as its fair value by an independent auctioneer.

TELFER INDUSTRIAL GROUP

Introduction

Telfer Industrial Group comprises Telfer Holdings Limited and its subsidiary companies. In your capacity as Group Financial Accountant you are currently reviewing the draft consolidated financial statements of the group. The Finance Director has requested that you prepare a memorandum outlining any issues which may require amendment.

During your review of the financial statements, the following matters have been brought to your attention:

(1) Acquisition of Summit Limited

On 31 May 2x07 the parent company, Telfer Holdings Limited, purchased 25% of Summit Limited. Telfer Holdings Limited had board representation in Summit Limited at that time, and was able to exercise significant influence over that company. Summit Limited is a producer and distributor of a high margin industrial component, and Telfer's shareholding gives the group a presence in an important and expanding market.

The 25% stake in Summit Limited was acquired for cash consideration of €2.5 million. The identifiable assets less liabilities of Summit Limited at that time were included in its statement of financial position at €7 million.

On the 31 May 2x08, Telfer Holdings Limited acquired a further 65% of the shares in Summit Limited for a cash payment of €7.8 million. The identifiable assets less liabilities included in the statement of financial position of Summit Limited at that date amounted to €8 million. The fair value of these net assets was €9 million. At 31 May 2x08, the fair value of Telfer's previous 25% shareholding in Summit was €2.3 million.

Acquisition costs of €200,000 were incurred by Telfer Holdings Limited in connection with the purchase of the controlling stake on the 31 May 2x08.

On the 28 February 2x09, Telfer Holdings Limited sold 20% of the shares in Summit Limited for cash proceeds of €3 million.

It is group policy to value non-controlling interest at its proportionate share of the subsidiary's fair value of identifiable net assets.

In their separate/individual financial statements, companies within the group account at cost for investments in subsidiaries, joint ventures and associates.

Ignore taxation.

(2) Property asset

Rampton Limited is a wholly owned subsidiary of Telfer Holdings Limited. On the 1 June 2x06 Rampton Limited purchased a building at a cost of €2 million for use as an administrative office by company personnel. The property was revalued to €2.5 million at the 31 May 2x07.

The property proved to be surplus to requirements, following staff relocation, and in May 2x08 it was decided to dispose of it at the earliest opportunity. At the 31 May 2x08, the property was classified as being held for sale. At that date, the market value was €3 million, and selling costs were estimated at €100,000.

At the 31 May 2x09, the property was valued at €1.8 million, net of selling costs, and it was withdrawn from sale at that date, due to a scarcity of buyers. The value in use of the building at that time was estimated at €1.5 million.

Rampton Limited depreciates property over 50 years on a straight line basis.

Ignore taxation.

(3) Intra-group sales

During the year ended 31 May 2x09, Rampton purchased goods from Brink Limited, in which Telfer Holdings Limited held a 75% shareholding. These goods were supplied by Brink Limited at €12 million, inclusive of a mark-up of 25%.

One-third of these goods was held as inventory by Rampton Limited at the 31 May 2x09. All companies in the Telfer Group pay corporation tax at 20%, six months after their year end.

(4) Sale of goods

In May 2x09, Rampton Limited sold 10 units of its main product, an integrated waste management system. The selling price of each unit was €100,000, which included a profit margin of 20%. Two months' credit was allowed to purchasers of nine of the waste management systems, these terms being standard in the industry.

One customer was allowed an interest-free credit period of one year. The market rate of interest for financing this type of product is 10% per annum.

The draft financial statements of Summit Limited for the year ended 31 May 2x09 are included in Appendix I.

The Group financial statements have also been prepared in draft form in Appendix II below.

Requirement:

You are required to draft a memorandum to the Finance Director of the Telfer Group, outlining your recommendations in respect of the accounting issues as follows:

(1) Acquisition and disposal of shares in Summit Limited

(i)   *In respect of the 25% acquisition of shares on the 31 May 2x07:*

- Outline the appropriate accounting treatment and provide the necessary journal entries, in the financial statements of the Telfer Group.

(4 marks)

(ii)   *In respect of the 65% acquisition of shares on the 31 May 2x08:*

- Advise on the appropriate accounting treatment, provide the necessary journal entries, and prepare the disclosure note for inclusion in the financial statements of the Telfer Group.

(15 marks)

(iii) *In respect of the disposal of 20% of the shares of Summit Limited on the 28th February 2x09*

- Outline the appropriate accounting treatment and provide the necessary journal entries in the financial statements of the Telfer Group.

(5 marks)

(2) Property asset

- Outline the recommended accounting treatment *and* provide the journal entries in the financial statements of Rampton Limited for the years ending 31 May 2x07, 2x08 and 2x09. Ignore taxation.

(11 marks)

(3) Intra-group sales

(i) Outline the appropriate accounting treatment and journal entries for this transaction in the financial statements of the Telfer Group at 31 May 2x09.

(4 marks)

(ii) Draft the relevant disclosure notes, if any, in the financial statements of the Group and the individual financial statements of Rampton Limited.

(4 marks)

(4) Sale of goods

(i) Outline the appropriate accounting treatment for the sale of goods by Rampton Limited.

(3 marks)

(ii) Provide the journal entries for these transactions in 2x09 and 2x10.

(4 marks)

Appendix I

Draft Financial Statements of Summit Limited

Draft Statement of Comprehensive Income for the year ended 31 May 2x09

	2x09 €'000	2x08 €'000
Revenue	11,800	
Cost of sales	(7,950)	
Gross profit	3,850	
Distribution costs	(300)	
Administrative expenses	(500)	
Other expenses	(400)	
Finance costs	(400)	
Profit before tax	2,550	
Income tax expense	(1,370)	
Profit for the year from continuing operations	1,180	
Other comprehensive income:		
Items that will not be reclassified to profit or loss:		
Gains on property revaluation	250	
Total comprehensive income for the year	1430	

Draft Statement of Financial Position of Summit Limited at 31 May 2x09

	Notes	2x09 €'000	2x08 €'000
Assets			
Non-current assets			
Land and buildings		5,451	
Plant and equipment		4,645	
		10,096	
Current assets			
Inventories of finished goods		1,469	
Trade and other receivables		1,395	
Cash and cash equivalents		1,155	
		4,019	
Total assets		14,115	
Liabilities			
Current liabilities			
Trade and other payables		2,215	
Income tax payable		1,350	
		3,565	
Non-current liabilities			
Term loan		820	
Provisions		300	
		1,120	
Total liabilities		4,685	
Net assets		9,430	
Equity			
Equity attributable to owners of the parent			
Share capital		100	
Share premium account		250	
Revaluation surplus		1,000	
Retained earnings		8,080	
Total equity		9,430	

Appendix II

Draft Consolidated Financial Statements of the Telfer Group

Draft Consolidated Statement of Comprehensive Income for the year ended 31 May 2x09

	2x09 €'000	2x08 €'000
Revenue	52,000	
Cost of sales	(27,950)	
Gross profit	24,050	
Distribution costs	(4,800)	
Administrative expenses	(10,500)	
Finance costs	(620)	
Profit before tax	8,130	
Income tax expense	(2,150)	
Profit for the year from continuing operations	5,980	
Other comprehensive income		
Items that will not be reclassified to profit or loss:		
Gains on property revaluation	1,400	
Total comprehensive income for the year	7,380	
Profit attributable to:		
Owners of the parent	5,550	
Non-controlling interests	430	
	5,980	
Total comprehensive income attributable to:		
Owners of the parent	6,950	
Non-controlling interests	430	
	7,380	

Draft Statement of Financial Position of the Telfer Group at 31 May 2x09

	Notes	2x09 €'000	2x08 €'000
Assets			
Non-current assets			
Property, plant and equipment		27,750	
Investment Property		4,000	
Goodwill		3,800	
		35,550	
Current assets			
Inventories		3,444	
Investments		1,000	
Trade and other receivables		3,395	
Cash and cash equivalents		2,155	
		9,994	
Total assets		45,544	
Liabilities			
Current liabilities			
Trade and other payables		6,965	
Income tax payable		4,150	
		11,115	
Non-current liabilities			
Convertible debentures		1,600	
Term loan		2,120	
Provisions		3,400	
		7,120	
Total liabilities		18,235	
Net assets		27,309	

Equity
Equity attributable to owners of the parent

Share capital	1,000
Share premium account	1,700
Revaluation surplus	3,904
Other reserves	900
Retained earnings	17,205
	24,709
Non-controlling interests	2,600
Total equity	27,309

CAMPBELL GROUP

Introduction

You have recently been appointed as Financial Accountant for the Campbell Group of companies, which has a growing presence in the automobile and ancillary services sector. The Campbell Group, which is listed on the Dublin and London stock exchanges, is headed up by its parent company, Campbell Holdings Limited. There are also a number of subsidiary companies, most of which are wholly owned by Campbell Holdings Limited. Group strategy has been to form a separate company for each main area of operation, and currently there are individual subsidiaries responsible for car sales, car hire, valeting and repairs, leasing and hire purchase, and sales of motor accessories.

You have received a file from the Chief Accountant, Martin Mangan, which contains the following information:

- Matters arising from the 2x10 audit of the Group   (Appendix I below)
- Draft consolidated financial statements for the year ended 31 December 2x10.   (Appendix II below)

Requirements:

On the basis of the information provided by the Chief Accountant, draft a memorandum to Martin Mangan, outlining:

(1) The earnings per share figures of the Group for the year ended 31 December 2x10 (including the 2x09 comparative).

(2) The accounting treatment for employee benefits for the year ended 31 December 2x10. See detailed requirement in Appendix I below. It should be assumed that the EPS computations in (1) above will not be affected by any adjustments required in this section.

(3)   What additional disclosures are required by international accounting standards, in view of the fact that the ordinary shares of the Campbell Group are listed on the Dublin and London stock exchanges.

Appendix I

Matters arising from the 2x10 audit of the Campbell Group

(1) Share Capital

On the 31 December 2x09, the Campbell Group had 800 million issued ordinary shares of €1 par value. There were €200 million of 10% irredeemable preference shares in issue at the same date. There had been no change in issued share capital during the year ended 31 December 2x09.

The following additional ordinary shares were issued during the year ended 31 December 2x10:

(i)   On the 1 January, the Group announced a one for four rights issue at €2 per share. The exercise date was the 1 February, and the market price immediately before the exercise date was €2.50.

(ii)   On the 1 April, the Campbell Group issued 200 million ordinary shares for cash at full market price of €2.45.

(iii) On the 1 July, the Group made a one for one bonus issue.

(iv)   On the 1 October, the Group purchased 100 million treasury shares for cash of €2.50 per share. This was the market price at that date.

The following issues also relate to the ordinary shares of the Campbell Group:

–   On the 1 April 2x10, share options were issued to 10 executives in the Campbell Group. Each executive had the option to purchase 20 million ordinary shares for an exercise price of €2 per share. The average market price of the ordinary shares during 2x10 was €2.50.
    The exercise rights for each executive are dependent on completing three years of service with the Campbell Group up to 31 March 2x13.

–   The 8% Convertible Debentures are convertible into ordinary shares in 2x12 at the rate of 50 shares per €100 of convertible loan stock.

–   The Campbell Group pays corporation tax at 30%.

(2) Employee Benefits

(a) Short-term employee benefits

In December 2x10 a problem with the payroll system in one of the Campbell Group subsidiaries, Auto Limited, has meant that no record of payroll costs has been made for the entire month. Details of wages and salaries in that subsidiary for December are as follows:

	€'M
Wages and salaries (net)	10.4
PAYE	3.6
Employer's PRSI	1.1
Holiday pay	0.8
Medical insurance provided for staff	0.6
	16.5 (Note 1)

Note 1: €1.2M relates to costs incurred in the construction of a new factory extension. With the exception of wages and salaries of €10.4M, none of the above amounts were paid at 31 December 2x10.

The Campbell Group also pays an annual staff bonus of €2,000 to all employees who provide a minimum of ten months of service during the year, and who are employees of the Group at 31 December. Auto Limited had a total of 1,000 employees at 31 December 2x10, of whom 900 had worked 10 months or more during the year.

(b) Post-employment benefits

(i) Defined contribution plan
The Campbell Group operates a defined contribution pension plan for employees who commenced employment with the Group on or after 1 January 2x07. Under the plan, post-employment benefits will be based on the returns on employer and employee contributions. Required contributions for the Campbell Group for the year ended 31 December 2x10 amounted to €120M, of which €25M was outstanding at the year end. Employee contributions for the same period were €40 million, which have been paid in full.

No accounting entries have been made in respect of these contributions.

(ii) Defined benefit plan

The Campbell Group operates a defined benefit pension plan for employees who commenced employment with the Group prior to the 1 January 2x07. The pension scheme is non-contributory.

At 31 December 2x09, the Campbell Group recorded a defined benefit liability of €600million, comprising the following items:

	€'m
Present value of defined benefit obligation	1,680
Fair value of plan assets	1,080
Defined benefit liability	600

The following information relates to the year ended 31 December 2x10:

	€'m
Employer contributions	400
Benefits paid	150
Net interest cost (Note 1)	20
Current service cost	390
Present value of defined benefit obligation at year end	2,300
Fair value of assets of plan at year end	1,650

No accounting entries have been made in the year ended 31 December 2x10.

Note 1: Net interest cost comprises:

Interest income on plan assets	€210m*
Interest cost on defined benefit obligation	€230m

* This is the expected return on the plan's assets.

Requirements:

(i) Defined contribution plan

Calculate the expense for the year ended 31 December 2x10, and the liability at 31 December 2x10.

(ii) Defined benefit plan

Calculate the defined benefit expense for the year ended 31 December 2x10, and the defined benefit liability at 31 December 2x10.

Appendix II

Draft Statement of Financial Position of the Campbell Group
as at 31 December

	31 December 2X10 €'m	31 December 2X09 €'m
Non-current assets		
Tangible Assets	8,620	6,000
Investments	1,000	
	9,620	6,000
Current assets		
Inventory	800	1,000
Trade receivables	2,200	2,000
Cash	300	200
	3,300	3,200
Total assets	12,920	9,200
Equity and liabilities		
Current liabilities		
Trade and other payables	2,167	1,700
Bank overdraft	2,400	2,000
	4,567	3,700
Non-current liabilities		
Pension liability	600	600
8% Convertible Debentures	500	500
Total liabilities	5,667	4,800
Equity		
Share capital (Note 1)	2,600	1,000
Share premium	1,490	1,000
Equity reserve	33	–
Revaluation surplus	1,100	700
Retained Earnings	1,230	1,500
	6,453	4,200
Non-controlling interests	800	200
Total equity (Note 2)	7,253	4,400
Total equity and liabilities	12,920	9,200

Note 1: Share Capital

	31 December 2x10 €'m	31 December 2x09 €'m
Ordinary shares of €1	2,400	800
10% Irredeemable Cumulative Preference Shares	200	200
	2,600	1,000

Note 2: Statement of Changes in Equity

	OSC	10% Pref Shares	Share Premium	Equity Reserve	Retained Earnings	Revaluation Surplus	NCI	Total Equity
	€'m	€'m	€'m	€'m	€'m	€'m	€'m	€'m
Bal. @ 1/1/2x10	800	200	1,000	–	1,500	700	200	4,400
Rights issue	200		200					400
Issue at fair value	200		290					490
Bonus issue	1,200				(1,200)			
Treasury shares					(250)			(250
Share Option Scheme				33				
Total comprehensive income					1,200	400	600	2,200
Preference dividend					(20)			(20
Bal. @ 31/12/2x10	2,400	200	1,490	33	1,230	1,100	800	7,253

Draft Statement of Comprehensive Income of the Campbell Group
for the Year Ended 31 December

	2X10 €'m	2X09 €'m
Revenue	12,600	10,200
Cost of sales	7,880	6,800
Gross profit	4,720	3,400
Administration costs	1,200	1,000
Distribution costs	1,020	850
Finance costs	150	400
Profit before tax	2,350	1,150
Income tax expense	550	200
Profit for the year	1,800	950

Other comprehensive income:		
Items that will not be reclassified to profit or loss:		
Revaluation gains	400	250
Total comprehensive income for the year	2,200	1,200

	2x10 €'m	2x09 €'m
Profit attributable to:		
Owners of the parent	1,200	870
Non-controlling interests	600	80
	1,800	950
Total comprehensive income attributable to:		
Owners of parent	1,600	1,120
Non-controlling interests	600	80
	2,200	1,200

INDEX

WELCOME TO
MEETINGS NOT STARTING
WITHOUT YOU

Chartered Accountants work at the highest levels in Irish business. In fact six out of ten Irish Chartered Accountants work at Finance Director level or above.

Discover our flexible training options:
CharteredCareers.ie

Chartered Accountants Ireland